RESTORING
A HOME IN ITALY

Twenty-two

Home Owners

Realize

Their Dream

ELIZABETH HELMAN MINCHILLI

Photographs by
SIMON MCBRIDE

 ARTISAN | NEW YORK

Published by Artisan
A Division of Workman Publishing Company, Inc.
708 Broadway New York, New York 10003
www.artisanbooks.com

Library of Congress Cataloging-in-Publication Data

Helman Minchilli, Elizabeth
    Restoring a home in Italy / Elizabeth Helman
Minchilli ; photographs by Simon McBride.
        p. cm.
    Includes bibliographical references.
    ISBN 1-57965-172-0
    1. Architecture, Domestic—Conservation and
restoration—Italy. 2. Interior architecture—Italy. I.
McBride, Simon. II. Title.

NA7355 .H45 2001
728'.0942'028—DC21

2001034311

PRINTED IN ITALY

10 9 8 7 6 5 4 3 2 1

FIRST PRINTING

Book design by Susi Oberhelman

IN LOVING MEMORY OF ENZO MINCHILLI (1915–2001),
WHO INHERITED HIS PASSION FOR THE WAY THINGS
ARE BUILT FROM HIS FATHER, AND PASSED IT ON TO HIS SON—
AND SO TO ME. THIS BOOK IS FOR HIM.

CONTENTS

INTRODUCTION

The most revealing research for this book was restoring our own house in Umbria. Seeing it today covered in climbing roses, it's hard to recall the pile of stones it once was.

MY LOVE AFFAIR WITH ITALY has deep roots. No, my ancestors weren't Italian. My introduction to Italian life came about much more abruptly. After passing a fairly uneventful first twelve years of my life in St. Louis, Missouri, I came back from summer camp one August to find that my parents had rented out our house, sold their business, and were in the process of packing us up to move to Rome, which they had visited for the very first time while I was away.

Despite the initial trepidation any twelve-year-old would feel, it didn't take me long to settle into the Italian way of life. We moved into an ancient palazzo in the city's historic center, and I was allowed to wander the city on my own, such was the safety of Rome at the time. Maybe it was the sudden freedom I was given. Maybe it was that I was at such an impressionable age. Whatever the reason, it added up to my forming a lasting love affair with all things Italian.

After two years in Rome, and traveling the country on family holidays, we moved back to the United States. Although we continued to come back for vacations, I was always trying to devise a more permanent solution: a summer studying Italian in Florence, two years living in a Florentine attic while researching my dissertation on Renaissance gardens in the archives at the Uffizi. I felt truly at home only within the sights, smells, and welcoming embrace of Italy. Finally, my appointment with destiny came in the form of love—of course. I met my husband, Domenico, an Italian architect, and settled for good in the country where I knew I belonged.

As an architectural historian, I studied buildings and gardens, and I saw my share of Medici villas and papal estates. I worked in the archives, pouring over dusty lists and inventories, plans and drawings, reconstructing palatial residences from centuries before in my mind. The work Domenico was doing—restoring abandoned farmhouses and bringing them lovingly back to life—was something completely new for me. I have

to admit that my eyes had never lingered on the crumbling farmhouses that dotted the countryside. If they weren't on my historic or academic itinerary, I hadn't considered them one way or another.

That was all to change, of course, as I began to take an interest in Domenico's projects. Eventually, I became intimately familiar with the language of restoration. My Italian is fluent today, but when it comes to vocabulary I feel much more comfortable talking about beams and plaster than, say, hemlines or the latest movie.

I learned pretty early on that there are as many reasons, or even rationalizations, for turning ruins into homes as there are home owners. Most people have very romantic and emotional explanations: a love affair with the light or the way of life in Italy, a desire to sink down roots in a country that has a history stretching back thousands of years. Some people want to make wine, others want to escape. The motivations are endless, and endlessly fascinating.

But what I found most gripping was the actual nuts and bolts of turning crumbling walls into a real home. And over the years, based on the steady stream of questions both Domenico and I get, I realized that most people have absolutely no idea of the work involved in achieving that end.

This book is an attempt to fill in the blanks. I hope it answers some of the major questions and eliminates much of the confusion. I've traveled the length and breadth of

Italy and have chosen a wide range of homes and home owners to showcase here.

Since this is Italy, there are no rules to follow, except for those that guide your heart. These are homes that were created with love, and often against all odds. What does it take to imagine a warm hearth while you're looking at a pile of cold stones? How do you even begin to picture a table set for a Sunday lunch when sheep have been the most recent residents? Of course, this is part of the charm, and the magic. This is what I hope to convey in *Restoring a Home in Italy*.

The pergola off the kitchen, above, is covered in Virginia creeper, which turns a bright red in the autumn. This area, which is also shaded by an ancient elm tree, is where we spend most of our time in the summer.

NORTHWEST

LIGURIA

UP UNTIL TWENTY YEARS AGO the area north of the Gulf of Spezia, called Cinque Terre, was practically inaccessible to all but the most dedicated tourist. The five towns— Vernazza, Riomaggiore, Manarola, Monterosso al Mare, and Corniglia, perched on the cliff overlooking the gulf—were reachable only by foot or by boat. At one time, this steep, inhospitable land was intensely cultivated. Stone retaining walls created a system of terraces for crops and farmsteads. While farming has declined, the terraces still produce a well-known white wine, and excellent olive oil is coaxed from the wind-twisted, silver-gray olive trees.

Eventually train tracks were laid, and the humble villages were discovered. Now, two decades

THE CELLAR, WHICH IS NOW the summer living room, was carved
out of living rock and is partly sunken into the face of the cliff. The French doors lead
out to the terrace. The dining room, above, part of the self-contained apartment, is heated
in winter by a wood-burning stove. The blue of the walls was created using an old recipe:
copper sulfate crystals (also used to protect grapevines from fungus) were mixed with
water and lime. Getting the correct proportions was crucial, as too much copper turns the
paint violet. Previous spread: The house's most distinctive feature—its pink exterior—
re-creates the original color, faded and mottled by sea salt and sun.

later, a road does pass through the area, but
reaching many of the farmhouses still requires
a passion for hiking ancient mule paths!

It was during a ramble along the upper
path overlooking the sea that an English
couple stopped for a drink along the way at
the one bar in Prevo. Chatting with the owner,
they discovered that the empty pink house
next door was indeed abandoned and had
been on the market for some time. Seduced
by the setting and taking no heed of the

possible problems of converting the place into a vacation home, the couple were soon the newest residents of the upper corniche.

Through mutual friends, they found architect Sebastiano Brandolini, who was willing to take a look at their restoration project. Instead of finding the house in "quite good shape and only needing painting and maybe a bathroom or two," as the owners thought, he found a house hanging on for dear life to the edge of a cliff, with roof tiles and bricks cascading down at the slightest touch.

Logistics—getting workers and materials to the site—would dictate architectural decisions and become part of the design itself. Several local contractors declined the job; the prospect of organizing the work and accessing the site was too daunting. Although today there is a fairly good road that comes within 300 meters of the house, at the time there was only a small dirt path. One contractor proposed using mules to speed things up.

The restoration took about a year. The architect estimates that at least 50 percent of the manpower was used just to carry rubble out and up the steep path and to haul new materials in. But when it came to laying the foundations for the panoramic terrace, he

THE TOP FLOOR, above left, reached by an external staircase, is reserved for guest bedrooms. A picture-perfect view of the nearby town of Corniglia is framed by the window. Like all the rooms in the house, the master bathroom, below left, faces the sea. The tub was positioned to take in the view. Opposite: "I tried to be as stingy as possible when dealing with the details," says the architect. "The house was originally very simple, mostly because of the poverty of the owners. I've tried to retain this minimal feel."

came up with a unique, thoroughly modern solution. To avoid more than two weeks of continuous trips up and down the hill with wheelbarrows to cart cement from a mixer perched on the edge of the cliff, the mixer was parked slightly higher up. When the cement was ready, a helicopter swooped down, loaded up, and dumped its load— two tons—onto the terrace. The whole operation took only half an hour, more than offsetting the cost of renting the helicopter.

The house, which serves as a summer retreat, is simple in design, almost to the point of being monastic. Often lent to friends, it's easy to open up and use, even after being closed for several months at a time. A self-contained apartment on the top level is heated separately and can be easily used during in winter. The furnishings throughout have been kept to a bare minimum, and the purpose of each room is pretty loosely defined. Beds and sofas get moved around, a living room becomes a bedroom, and so on.

For the most part, life is lived outside, overlooking the magnificent views, which change with the weather and light throughout the day. Since the house is built into the side of the cliff, the windows all face toward the sea. An outside staircase connects the two main floors, and the steps become another outdoor living space. The two terraces, heavily planted with lavender and bougainvillea, jut out over the expanse of blue. ■

THE HOUSE ACTS as a sundial, with the views and vistas changing as the sun arcs across the sky through the day. The terraces, loggias, garden, and staircases, which seem to hang out over the cliff, are an integral part of the restoration, and some of the most popular spots in the house.

POSIZIONE

Breathtaking views don't always translate into easy access. The cliff-hugging house in Prevo, below and right, was restored with great effort; stone terracing, which supported the paths, had crumbled away, and rebuilding the stone walls was one of the first tasks.

Location, location, location: we think we know what the expression means—an apartment on Fifth Avenue is worth more than one in Brooklyn, a townhouse in Knightsbridge is worth more than a cottage in the Cotswolds. In Italy, however, location is a bit more complicated. Certainly some areas are more desirable than others. Tuscany has long attracted foreigners and Italians alike, and recently Todi, in Umbria, has become "hot." But specific locations within even coveted areas present their own problems. "Many attractive homes with splendid views are so inaccessible as to make them virtually uninhabitable," says architect Sebastiano Brandolini. While he was able to work miracles in the house at Prevo, there are many others nearby, perched on the edges of cliffs, that remain untouched. Ancient terraced paths that once provided access to them have long since fallen into disrepair, and even if they had survived the centuries, they would be unsuitable for modern-day construction equipment.

In Venice, rubble is carried out and materials brought in by boat. "When you plan a project in Venice," says architect Gretchen Alexander, "you have to factor in how many boatloads of rubble and materials you can move a day. This involves looking at the tide charts, figuring out capacity and depth. It becomes quite complicated and usually adds at least an extra six to eight months to what a similar job would have taken on *terra ferma*!"

A VILLA ON

LAGO MAGGIORE

VISITING LAGO MAGGIORE, the biggest body of water in Italy's lake district, is like entering a fairy tale. The flat, glistening surface of the water reflects incredibly verdant gardens backed by wooded hills and mountains. Every so often a town appears on the coastline, and villas rise up nearby. The changeable weather makes it all the more dramatic: Rainstorms give way to sunshine in the blink of an eye. Like all of the lakes in northern Italy, Lago Maggiore is incredibly romantic, and the abundance of water makes the landscape rich and lush—very different from the rugged, sun-drenched hills of central Italy that I'm accustomed to.

Ghislaine and Annibale Brandolini d'Adda decided that this setting would be the perfect place to raise a family; Milan was beginning to feel too urban by far. They bought their new lakeside home virtually sight unseen—Annibale took one look at the overgrown garden and immediately decided to buy before he had even seen the house itself.

The house had charm of its own as well. The structure probably dates back to the late seventeenth or early eighteenth century.

AN EXTERNAL STAIRCASE LEADS from the ground level of the courtyard to the balcony, left, which runs around one and a half sides. The patterned paving tiles of cast cement were installed by the previous owner. Art nouveau decoration beneath the cornice, above, has been carefully restored using the original colors. The gutters harness the rainwater and lead to a cistern, where it is collected and used in the garden. Previous spread: Although the home owners accomplished miracles by restoring the main villa in only four months, they have been working on the rest of the property in stages. The neo-Gothic wing, on the left (*il castelletto,* or "little castle") will be a home office once the central heating system is extended.

THE COURTYARD, above, although cleaned and restored, remains almost as it was when the Brandolinis bought the house. The terra-cotta tiles under the portico and the checkerboard-patterned tiles were left intact. The only change was the installation of a row of rectangular slabs of gray beola as a border. The portico off the courtyard, opposite, is used as an outdoor dining area almost year-round in the temperate lakeside microclimate. The staircase in the background leads to the second-floor balcony.

An inner, cloisterlike courtyard indicates that the building was originally a monastery. At the turn of the twentieth century, it was bought by Maurice Blondel, a well-known French botanist at the Sorbonne, who decided to create an experimental garden along the temperate lake.

By the time the Brandolinis bought the property, the garden was in a sad state of abandon, and most of the changes to the

house had been superficial. Luckily, the structure itself was in fairly good shape; the roof and walls were all doing their jobs. But a major revamping of the electrical, plumbing, and water management systems was in order. Architects Giuseppe Ferrari and Sebastiano Brandolini, Annibale's brother, were hired to do a high-quality modernization at minimal cost—and to do it in four months.

In the kitchen, modernity and practicality reign in an atmosphere of tasteful minimalism. Italians tend to keep kitchens small and basic, focusing their attention on more public areas such as the living room and dining room. Ghislaine, who is Dutch, wanted a kitchen in which the whole family could gather. The new room is the biggest in the

MOST OF THE KITCHEN ELEMENTS, left, are sleek and thoroughly modern and come from a well-known Italian kitchen manufacturer. White Carrara marble from Tuscany forms the countertop. More old-fashioned is the wood-burning grill, set into the wall and framed in pink granite from Bavena. Seen through a window, the central courtyard, above, is almost an extension of the kitchen, with two windows and a pair of large French doors connecting the two spaces.

house, the eating and cooking areas separated only by an open archway. One of its most striking features is the stone floor, which replaced the ceramic tiles put in by the previous owner. Giant slabs of beola, a gray stone from the nearby quarry at Bavena, were laid to create an almost sculptural effect. The architect visited the quarry daily, making sure that each stone was hand-cut to size and numbered to correspond to his floor plan.

While the house takes in sweeping views over the garden and toward the lake, it also has a private inner courtyard. Neoclassical

A DINING AREA is included in the open space of the living room, above, and the entire room is paved in cherrywood parquet. The fireplace, probably installed in the last century, is framed in pink marble from Bavena. The home owners had the inner frame painted to mimic the marble. Large bunches of hydrangeas come straight from the garden. The living room, right, is the most formal room in the house. Large plate-glass doors give views of the garden and, beyond, the lake.

columns surround this *cortile*, and checker-board tiles, installed by the previous owner, provide a carpetlike effect. The nineteenth-century painted frieze and decorative panels above the cornice have been meticulously restored. Because the house has a creek running beneath it, the paints were carefully selected to "breathe" so humidity could escape and not blister the surfaces.

The upper floors are reached either via the courtyard staircase or an internal staircase near the kitchen. The bedrooms, paved in the original pine planking, have floor-to-ceiling French doors, all the better to look out toward the garden and lake.

The most challenging aspect of the restoration was water management. This entailed first creating a sewage system (there was none) and separating the clean running water from that destined for the sewer. The clean water was then harnessed to bring the garden back to life.

Every summer a group of students from the Dutch Groene Delta College Rijswijk come down to help resurrect Blondel's origi-nal creation. Ghislaine welcomes the challenge and takes her work to heart. "We've tried to respect the house and garden," she says. "In the end, we're just temporary visitors. I want to make sure that they're properly kept for future generations." ■

THE GUEST SUITE, above left, takes up the entire third floor. A mirrored closet door at the foot of the bed and built-in cabinetry beyond are all original. French doors in the second-floor master bedroom, below left, allow a perfect view of the lake from the bed. Here, as in the rest of the house, the color scheme was kept to a simple navy blue and white.

PROFESSIONISTI

As a rule, real estate agents don't have exclusives on any properties, so if you engage several, you may end up seeing the same house more than once. On the other hand, there are no officially shared listings, so you may miss out on something if you don't use their services. They generally charge from 3 to 10 percent of the selling price, split evenly between the buyer and the seller, although this figure is often open to negotiation. *Make sure you settle on a rate before you are shown anything.*

Many architects will help you find your house by weeding out unlikely properties with agents, visiting properties to narrow your choice, or reviewing a property before you sign any papers. While no one will provide guarantees, architects can usually spot unsolvable or costly problems such as severe structural flaws or ground erosion. That quaint building down the road may be a chicken farm that brings an overwhelming poultry smell when the wind blows south.

A notary, *notaio,* acting as the representative of the government in property transactions, will draw up the deed and research any liens or other pending legal actions on the place you're buying. (Barring very complicated situations, it's generally not necessary to involve a lawyer in property transactions.) Try not to use a notary recommended by either the seller or the real estate agent; find someone neutral, even someone in another town, to assure complete impartiality. The notary charges a fixed fee of 2.5 percent of the official registered selling price of the property.

Some brave people choose to act as their own designers and site supervisors. This is fine if you understand that this will be a full-time job for a year or so and if you're familiar with the language and construction methods. Agents often recommend that you use a local surveyor, called a *geometra,* to oversee the restoration. His degree comes from a trade school, not from a university, but under Italian law he's qualified to design buildings up to a certain size. Many people are under the mistaken impression that his fees are lower than an architect's. Some people also mistakenly think that you need to hire someone "local" to grease the wheels to receive the necessary permits.

It's a much better idea, in my opinion, to hire a professionally trained architect with experience restoring these types of houses. Call me biased (I *am* married to such a person), but I truly feel that most restoration projects need professional guidance. The *geometra* is perfectly capable of drafting plans and applying for permits, but his training can't compare to the five years of university-level education, involving design and history studies, required for an architect's degree. It takes a bit more effort to find an architect, but it pays off in the end when you wind up with the house you've been dreaming of, not the *geometra*'s idea of what a restored farmhouse should be. (There's an Italian term, *casa di geometra,* referring to a modern and unfortunately unattractive home designed by a local *geometra.*)

"FOR ME THIS IS NOT JUST A HOUSE, but a garden with a house—you can't separate the two things," says Ghislaine. The garden, above, is slowly being restored to its turn-of-the-twentieth-century design. Luckily, many of the original plants remain, including the large camphor tree at the left, the oldest such example on the lake. The covered loggia that opens up off the third floor, opposite, takes in some of the best views of the garden, all the way down to the lake and the Borromean Islands.

A CONVENT IN

LOMBARDY

SINCE THE PHILOSOPHY OF recycling is predominant in Katrin Arens's furniture making, I wasn't surprised to find that she had chosen to "recycle" an abandoned convent into her home. In fact, the large three-story building on the Adda River near Bergamo had seen many reincarnations since it was built in the sixteenth century. The story goes that Leonardo da Vinci, who worked just down the river, designed the stone house; since the layout of the rooms, which are all interconnecting, reflects his design philosophy, it may just be true. At the time, the building boasted a large water mill, which powered the stones used to grind grain. The wheel eventually was dismantled and the mill transformed into a convent.

By the time Katrin discovered Il Mulino di Sotto—"The Lower Mill," as her house is called—one wing had been empty for five years and the other occupied by farmers. (Tenants still occupy that wing.) Katrin, her husband, and their three-year-old daughter took up residence on the second floor of the abandoned part of the building and located Katrin's business on the ground level. When they moved in, they had no electricity, no

THE HOME OWNER'S DESIGN OFFICE, opposite, is on the second floor. The bookshelves, part of her Terracielo (Earthsky) collection, were crafted out of salvaged wood. The kitchen, above, is the main room in the house; the wood-burning stove is used for cooking as well as heating the large space. Previous spread: The family lives on the second floor of the old mill, overlooking the river. The ground floor is devoted to the owner's furniture business; the attic remains abandoned—for now.

A LONG NARROW HALLWAY, above, bisects the apartment on the second floor. The space, overlooking the garden and river, serves as the living room and is furnished with the home owner's own designs. The floor, installed by the previous tenants, was left exactly as the home owners found it; the walls were simply whitewashed.

running water, and, of course, no heating. Katrin and her husband painted the walls, cleaned the place up, and camped out. When their daughter was born, a heating system was installed. Large aluminum tubes snake their way up the wall and across the ceiling, bringing heat generated from the boiler in the workshop, which is fueled with scraps left over from Katrin's work. But the overriding aim was to leave things as they were

RISCALDAMENTO

The aluminum pipes that run across Katrin Arens's second-floor apartment carry hot air from the wood-fueled boiler located in the woodworking shop on the ground floor.

To heat her home, which is located above the workshop where her furniture line is manufactured, Katrin Arens uses a boiler fueled by discarded wood chips. The hot air produced, which is pumped through shiny tubes, keeps both the house and workshop toasty throughout the winter months. Peter Pfefferkorn relies solely on old-fashioned fireplaces when the air gets chilly (see page 113). When the really cold weather sets in, he closes up his house until the following spring.

Most restorations of country homes, however, do involve the installation of a new heating system, generally powered by a furnace using either liquid gas or oil contained in external tanks. These tanks, 1,500 to 4,000 liters, usually sunk in the ground, are refilled on demand by private gas/fuel companies.

Another option is radiant, or floor, heating. It's finally catching on in Italy (it's more common in northern Europe), and for good reason: traditional systems in Italy rely on radiators, which take up wall and floor space and are not easy elements to incorporate into new decors. They often end up being placed under windows in niches, which are costly to dig out of stone walls. Radiant heating, which uses hot water run through plastic tubes under the floor, eliminates the radiator problem.

Surprisingly, solar heating is rare in Italy, a country where sunshine is plentiful and fuel expensive. It's been slow to catch on; the problem may be an aesthetic one: the solar panels are large, shiny, and modern looking, and finding an "invisible" yet efficient location for them is difficult.

as much as possible. The original handmade terra-cotta tiles are still in place in several of the rooms. The hallway flooring is cement, put down by the last tenants. The kitchen boasts the industrial tiles laid down by the farmers in the 1950s.

The house isn't "charming" in the way that most Italians think a country house should be. What makes the place a home are Katrin's creations. She designed almost all the

THE KITCHEN CABINETS, above, were designed by the home owner and built of plastered brick. Old pieces of wood, cut to size and hinged onto the supports, were fashioned into cupboard doors. A slab of cast concrete, polished smooth, forms the practical countertop. The plate rack hanging on the wall is a salvaged palette. Red industrial floor tiles, right, date from the 1950s. The shelves, also designed by the owner, are made of salvaged wood, sanded and polished to a soft finish.

furnishings, incorporating the wooden planks she "harvests" from construction sites. Heavy and rough to start with, the wood is cleaned and sanded down to display the softness and warmth that defines her aesthetic. The glowing tones of honey-colored woods stand out against the sparkling whitewashed walls. The cushions and mattresses that adorn her benches and chairs add softness to the decor.

It's not surprising that Katrin's furniture has enjoyed greater success in Germany than it has in Italy. Northern Europeans have a stronger tradition of recycling; Italians seem to want things either very new—ultra modern; or very old—antique. The idea of secondhand simply isn't part of the culture.

One of the main attractions of Il Mulino di Sotto is its location on the river. A green lawn flows from the back door down to the water. Here Katrin has set up tables and lounge chairs so that life can continue outside in the warm weather.

As Katrin's business expands, so do her plans for the house. She wants to take over the other half of the building when her neighbors move, and hopes one day to convert the attic space into extra rooms for storage and her new children's clothing line. ∎

MUCH OF THE HOUSE has elements dating from farmers' restorations in the 1950s and later. An exception is the beautiful sixteenth-century handmade terracotta tiles on the master bedroom floor, above and below left, which date from the building's days as a convent. The room looks out over the river from two large windows. Opposite: The owner designed several pieces of furniture for the garden, including a canopied platform. A tarp can be hung on the upper frame to provide a shady spot.

PIEDMONT

THE LANGHE IS A REGION IN

Piedmont better known for its food than its architecture. The area around Alba is world famous for white truffles, which are taken from the earth every fall. Vineyards, which stretch across the protected valleys, produce beloved Barolo wine. And groves of hazlenut trees yield the makings of myriad sweets and pastries, not to mention the ubiquitous Nutella.

Matteo Selvini and Katerina Weiss's converted farmhouse in the Langhe turned out to be one of the most original and interesting homes I visited during my research for this book. While most people try to rigorously maintain architectural and decorative elements of the original structures, this couple entrusted their restoration to the architectural innovations

of Giampiero Bosoni. His challenge was to turn a typical farmhouse into a weekend family home incorporating modern elements and comforts without totally erasing its original character.

The house itself was made up of two separate buildings, situated side by side on a hillside slope but with one half a story lower than the other. The part of the house facing the valley, with both levels above ground, was the stables and hayloft. The other half, with

THE KITCHEN, left—animal stalls in its first incarnation—takes up the front part of the ground floor. The door at the far end leads to a wooden deck. In the staircase leading from the kitchen to the upper levels, the first flight, from the kitchen to the bedrooms, above left, is made of smoothly polished concrete. The second flight, which leads to the living room, above right, is made of sheet iron and anchored to the wall with steel rods set with a silicon-based glue. Previous spread: The division between the two original adjacent buildings is clearly visible in the roofline. The house is faced with stone covered in plaster, as it was when it was first built.

the lower level partly below ground, was the farmhouse. A simple way to resolve the problem of the different levels would have been to completely gut the interiors. Instead, Giampiero chose to incorporate this difference into the new plan. A staircase connects the three levels and emphasizes them with a variety of design elements. The first flight of stairs, leading from the kitchen to the bedroom level, is made of polished concrete. The second flight, which leads from the bedroom level to the living room/hayloft, is made of polished steel.

As in most farmhouses, the relationship between exterior and interior was minimal. To increase the communication between them, two wooden decks were added. One is located off the new entrance to the master bedroom, on the long side of the house. The other is off the kitchen, extending this family room to the outside. Both decks are further emphasized by steel pergolas, which frame the surrounding landscape.

Three windows were created in the original hayloft upstairs. Large floor-to-ceiling openings existed in the old house, but the way in which they were converted into new windows makes a definite architectural statement. The frames, made of wood, project

THE SECOND-FLOOR living room, right, was once the hayloft of the barn. The fireplace, designed by the architect, is constructed of plastered bricks. In the living room and in the corridor and bedrooms, above left, the flooring is waxed larch planks. A dividing wall on the left was added to create a guest bedroom. Chestnut beams and panels of the roof, below left, were totally dismantled, cleaned, and reassembled exactly as they were in the original house.

THE MASTER SUITE, located at one end of the farmhouse, above, has a dressing room and full bath as well as its own separate entrance, which opens on to a small wooden deck topped by a vine-covered pergola. The niches in this room and the children's bedroom, opposite, above, were created by closing a connecting door between the two rooms. Wall colors throughout the house, carefully chosen by the owners, vary from room to room. The children's bathroom, opposite, below, owes its brightness to terrazzo tiles salvaged from the kitchen. A long industrial double sink was installed in favor of more traditional residential versions.

10 centimeters (4 inches) beyond the plane of the facade. Inside, the 5-centimeter (2-inch) thickness of the wood creates a step and defines the space created by the new windows. The glass is embraced by brightly painted red metal frames, creating an industrial rather than rural effect.

The hayloft, now used as the family room, had no windows opening to the valley below. The solution was to cut long, narrow floor-to-ceiling windows to frame the view in a new and unexpected way. Keeping them narrow was an aesthetic decision, but it turned out to be a less expensive one as well: the smaller the opening cut into the exisiting stone walls, the cheaper.

While most restorations aim to hide any additions, here new elements are highlighted and emphasized, often with color. All the new doors were painted bright blue, in contrast to the gray plaster of the facade. The shutters, also new, were painted a paler shade of blue. New niches in the master bedroom and children's room were painted bright cherry red.

The past isn't totally ignored. Salvaged materials are used in several places. The kitchen floor is paved with handmade antique terra-cotta tiles from another farmhouse in the area, and both bathrooms, located on the second floor, make use of the terrazzo marble tiles taken up from the old kitchen.

Many of the new elements of the house are gradually being adapted to family life. The geometrically rigid white pergolas, for example, are succumbing to the gardening instincts of the owners: bright pink roses and other climbers are snaking their way up and over the supports. And on weekends, when the family comes down from Milan, a Ping-Pong table takes pride of place on the large deck outside the kitchen. ■

FINESTRE

Most owners of Italian farmhouses opt for new windows, though some like the rickety charm of the original fittings. Peter Pfefferkorn was able to salvage all of his windows, substituting panes of glass only where necessary (see page 108). The Da Sies (see page 70) were also insistent on retaining the original frames wherever possible, going so far as to copy the old designs, even when they knew that a more modern window would be better at keeping the elements out.

Another decision is whether to open up new windows. Since most of the ground floors were once animal stalls, there's usually only a door opening and few windows, if any. Permission to create new window openings varies from town to town, with parts of the Tuscan countryside and most historic city centers being the most stringent.

It's often tempting to make new window openings very large. The Matés deliberately kept theirs small to remain more in keeping with the original house (see page 96). Giampiero Bosoni, the architect of the Selvini-Weiss house, opted for long but narrow windows along walls that were otherwise blind (see page 53).

In Italy, all windows must be special-ordered; standard-size ready-made windows don't exist. Wood is the traditional material for farmhouse windows; new ones have the advantage of being tightly made to keep out wind and rain and are usually double-glazed to insulate against heat and cold. Recently, more and more companies have begun offering options for roll-down screens.

Ground-floor animal stalls may have few windows, but they often have large open archways that acted as covered porches where farm equipment could be stored. These spaces can be converted into rooms by closing in the arches with glass and steel, which has a thinner and less obtrusive frame than wood and gives a light and airy feeling akin to that of a greenhouse or winter garden (see pages 88–89, 102–103).

Traditionally, exterior louvered shutters were used mostly in urban settings. For the most part, they were too expensive for poor farmers, though some country settings where the weather was particularly harsh, such as the cliffside house at Prevo, necessitated their use. More common in the farmhouses are shutters (*scuri*) on the inside of the windows, used to darken rooms.

Rather than go "fake rustic" in the Selvini-Weiss Piedmont home, the architect used brightly painted metal frames for the large hayloft windows, giving them a decidedly industrial look. More traditional Piedmont-style boxed frames were used on the ground floor.

TRANSFORMATIONS OF FARMHOUSES into vacation retreats always involve the creation of an outdoor space for leisure activities. Since original farmer tenants had very little free time to spend outdoors, these areas have to be created from scratch. Here the solution was to build a wooden deck that opens off the kitchen and takes in the view over the valley.

NORTHEAST

AN ATTIC IN
VENICE

EVERY RESTORATION PROJECT
in Italy presents its own set of hurdles. The first time
we visited our own ruin in Todi, there wasn't even a
road to lead us there, much less bring in the cement
trucks and cranes. In Liguria, the cliffside house was
so inaccessible that a helicopter had to be used to
airlift in materials. Even seemingly straightforward
jobs, such as Karen Wolman's in Torre Gentile, can
bring surprises never imagined. As the contractor
was operating a small backhoe in her backyard, he
felt resistance and heard metal scraping upon metal.
Rather than dig away, he got down to have a look. As
it turned out, the last inhabitant of Karen's house had
stored bombs from World War II in the old vegetable
garden! Digging stopped, the firemen were called

in, and Karen's place was rendered bombless. Although Gretchen Alexander, an American architect, didn't have unexploded bombs to deal with in her restoration of an attic apartment in Venice, she knew from the beginning that the job would present some unique challenges. Contessa Loredan, the owner of the Palazzo Barbarigo della Terrazza, a seventeenth-century palace on the Grand Canal, asked her to restore the building's roof and to design an apartment under the rafters.

THE DINING ROOM, above, is squeezed in between the supporting beams. Large wooden beams supporting the roof, opposite, were left exposed in the living room, and skylights were added to let in light. Previous spread: The palazzo is located directly on the Grand Canal, next to the historic Palazzo Pisani Morreta. The main entrance is the arched doorway on the canal; the only other entrance is via a narrow alleyway to the rear, so all construction material had to be brought in and out by boat.

Zoning and construction codes in Venice are notoriously rigid; up until thirty years ago, permits weren't issued to convert unused spaces into habitable apartments. All that changed in 1966, when the city suffered a devastating flood. Rising tides poured into most of the palazzos' ground floors, making them virtually uninhabitable. New laws were enacted that allowed owners to transfer the registered volume of their ground-floor living spaces to the hitherto ignored attics.

Even so, since Venice continues to carefully protect its patrimony, permission to convert these spaces isn't always a given. Each request is considered on the basis of specific needs and merit. In asking for permission, Gretchen emphasized the fact that such a conversion would help to preserve the entire building. Attics, which require an enormous amount of upkeep, are often left to rot, since most attention is focused on the water-damaged foundations. By converting the space into an apartment, she argued, the owners were preserving the building as well as eliminating a potential fire hazard.

Palazzo Barbarigo is five stories high, considered a tall building for Venice. The

EVERY INCH OF SPACE is put to use beneath the sloping roof of the attic apartment. Small windows in the bedroom and bath, above and below left, opened up under the cornice of the roof, frame views out over the rooftops of Venice. Mirrors in the bathroom reflect the light and visually extend the space. Small white mosaic tiles help keep the look uncluttered. Opposite: The owner of the palace rents out this apartment. The current tenant, a designer, has installed a desk and bookshelves in the space between two large beams and the sloping roof.

beams are appropriately massive, and the support structure is complicated. Like most attic spaces in the city, the structure under the roof was made of paper-thin *canuccia*, a mixture of straw and plaster. This waferlike layer was hung from the roof beams to provide the ceiling for the apartment below. The attic itself had no real supporting floor, as it was never intended to be used either for living or storage. Gretchen's brief, then, was to construct an entirely new living space between the beams.

The job was incredibly difficult. Even getting material to the building site was a challenge. As it was surrounded by water, there was no place to install a crane, so everything had to be brought up and down the stairs by hand. A long winding staircase and narrow alleyways outside (only 91 centimeters—41 inches—wide) made the job even more difficult. Although boats were used, their usefulness was extremely limited. (Often, in Venetian restorations, certain elements that appear to reflect aesthetic decisions are actually dictated by the restrictions of the site. For instance, a particularly narrow stairwell or alleyway may prohibit the installation of mirrors or windows beyond a certain size.)

The new apartment, located within the cagelike structure of beams, mirrors the floor plan of the apartments below it. The living room is situated in the center; the bedroom, bath, and kitchen open off this central space. Permission to add some new elements, such as skylights and dormer windows, was granted. The only external addition, the construction of an *altana*—a traditional Venetian roof terrace that rises above the roofline—was a more complicated matter. While it was assumed the palazzo had originally had one, the planning commission was opposed to the construction of a new one without concrete

THE KITCHEN IS AS EFFICIENT AS A SHIP'S galley in its compact design, opposite. Open metal shelving makes the most of the narrow space. Above: Since there was no room for an exhaust hood over the stovetop, the architect cut small windows in the ceiling that can be opened for ventilation.

confirmation. But while browsing through a rack of antique postcards, Gretchen found an eighteenth-century engraving showing the palace topped by a very prominent *altana*. This was all the proof she needed to get her permit.

The new *altana*, built entirely of wood, follows traditional lines. The deck, reached by a short flight of steps, is just big enough for a table and chairs and gives a fine view of boats drifting along the Grand Canal, as they have for centuries. ■

Licenze/Permessi

The hardest and scariest part of a restoration has nothing to do with mortar and stone. It has everything to do with securing the correct permits.

It would be a pleasure to be able to write down, clearly, the steps to follow for obtaining these precious pieces of paper. But since each city, town, and hamlet has its own building commission and its own arcane set of rules, each project presents a unique agenda. In addition, houses are classified at different levels of historical importance, depending on where they are and when they were built. If a house is located in a historic center of a city or village, chances are it falls under the aegis of the Ministero per i Beni Culturali, or Ministry of Cultural Patrimony. Proposed plans must first pass this national institution—which prohibits almost all changes to facades and scrutinizes every proposed design aspect. If a house is actually considered to be part of the country's patrimony, or *vincolato,* yet another step is added to the process. Before you actually buy the property, it must be offered to the government for first refusal. And while the Italian government barely has funds to maintain what it already owns and almost never acts on this option, it adds another stressful and time-consuming chapter to the saga.

While you're waiting for construction permits for your project in the countryside, it would make sense to use the time to clear the land around the ruin, examine the foundations, perhaps start to lay the groundwork for a road. But even this work requires a special permit, this time from the Comunità Montana, the body that oversees Italy's forests and woods and the land bordering them.

Finally, your request arrives at the desk of the local planning commission, whose decisions seem to be as unpredictable as Italian politics. This is where the owner of the home near Siena (see page 118) ran into trouble, since her addition would have added to the overall volume of the house. She was given permission only after the architect proved that the proposed loggia was in fact an element of the original building. The home owner on page 178 ran into similar opposition to his living room addition. His solution was to knock down another portion of the building and transfer that volume to the living room.

Venice poses its own unique obstacle course. Once plans are past the local building commission, they must still be approved by the Salvaguardia di Venezia, a special commission set up in the early 1970s to safeguard Venice's fragile and precious architectural patrimony.

Houses located in seismically unstable areas must obtain yet another permit. The plans must be drawn up according to rigid building codes that specify stabilization of the current building and methods to make any new construction earthquake-proof.

Architect Gretchen Alexander fought hard for the permit to build an *altana* on the top of Palazzo Barbarigo della Terrazza. Although small, it is the most important "room" in the home, adding an entirely different dimension to the attic apartment.

FRIULI

EVEN THOUGH FRIULI'S borders are barely an hour away from Italy's biggest attraction—Venice—this northeast corner of the country remains mostly undiscovered by tourists. The region abuts both Slovenia and Austria (it was for many years part of the Austro-Hungarian Empire) and is culturally and historically remote from the rest of Italy. In the south, near the city of Pordenone and nearer the Veneto, things do in fact feel more Venetian, but with decidedly and uniquely Friulian overtones. Yet for all the beauty of the landscape— vineyards alternating with canals, flat plains giving way to small, one-steeple towns—the owners of Casa del Practico, a recently restored house, admit that settling there was a pure act of love.

Though located in a tranquil area, the abandoned farmhouse that Annalise and Roberto Da Sie purchased didn't have much to offer in the way of architectural interest or views. But Annalise, who had grown up in the area, knew the house well from her childhood and couldn't resist fulfilling a dream of one day living there.

The Da Sies turned their energies to meticulously restoring the interior of the house, using antique woods as their major theme. Since the area isn't particularly known for its artisan traditions, they cast their nets around the countryside near Asolo and Montebelluno, some 30 kilometers to the west. Every element in the house, either restored or newly commissioned, is handmade, from windows and doors down to the hardware holding everything together.

Claudio Caramel, an architect and family friend, oversaw the major work. All the

ANTIQUE WOODEN DOORS, opposite, were painstakingly sought out by the owners. The door at the end of the hall leads to the staircase, which is closed off with doors at either end and walls on either side so that the separate levels can be heated more easily during the winter. In the ground-floor living room, above and below right, the windows are for the most part original; wrought-iron fixtures were restored and some glass panes were replaced. The mantelpiece was crafted from a salvaged antique beam placed on stone supports. Previous spread: The house, situated on a north-south axis, is very well ventilated and remains cool and breezy throughout the summer. The south-facing arches of the two-story hayloft have been left open to create a sort of indoor-outdoor living room, used mostly in the summer.

IN THE PANTRY, above left, eighteenth-century Neapolitan tiles were installed using local sand instead of the usual cement for a much richer color. The deep marble sink is used to rinse off vegetables from the garden. Above right and opposite: The traditional Friulian *larino* is in a nook off the kitchen. It projects out from the wall, giving off heat in three directions. Two cushioned benches provide seating.

walls and levels remain as they were, but the first floor, formerly the stables, had just packed dirt for flooring and had to be replaced. The dirt was dug up, new foundations were laid, and insulation and flooring installed. Since the zone is quite rainy and wet, the entire foundation was heavily weatherproofed.

Most of the house's bigger beams are original. Some, weighing over 450 pounds, were carefully taken down and cleaned by hand. The home owners had planned to sandblast the entire ceiling, beams and all, to clean away the centuries of grime. As it turned out, many of the smaller beams were beyond repair, and in the end the entire roof had to be disassembled and rebuilt with materials salvaged from other sites.

One of the focal points of this home is, of course, the kitchen. During the cold winter months, when the family spends most weekends here, the coziest place to be is beside the

THE HAYLOFT BECAME the most striking room in the house. The ceiling was dismantled and restored, and the arched windows that face the front of the house were left unglazed. The larger beams are original; the smaller ones were beyond salvation and were replaced by beams from a nearby house. Antique wood parquet floors and the wrought-iron railing were added. The stone wall, once detached from the rest of the house during an earthquake, was stabilized and then repointed with local river sand.

THE BED IN THE MASTER BEDROOM, right, was designed around an antique door that became the headboard. The rest of the bed was made by a carpenter from salvaged antique wood. Here, as in the rest of the house, a final layer of plaster was applied to the wall with a small spatula to achieve an uneven, textured look, eliminating the need for a final coat of paint. The master bath, above, is reached through a walk-in closet off the bedroom. The pedestal sinks are new; the cupboard, mirrors, and towel rack are antique finds. The shower is in an adjacent room of its own.

larino, the open-sided fireplace typical in Friuli. In the warm summer months, family life switches to the other end of the house, where a large, two-story hayloft was transformed into an indoor/outdoor living room. Large arches, an unusual architectural element in houses in the area, face west. They have been left open to the elements so the room becomes a breezy and cool retreat in summer. One original stone wall remains; it was repointed with *sabbia di possagna,* a sand

THE CERAMIC WOOD-BURNING STOVE in the study dates from the nineteenth century. It was in pieces when the home owners discovered it in an antiques shop; it now works perfectly. The heavy wooden door and hardware, part of the old house, lead to the hayloft.

gathered from a local river, and cement. Wood plays a major role here, too. Ceiling beams were taken down, cleaned, and replaced. The broad antique pine floor planks were laminated onto newer wood; this process retains the patina of old wood but eliminates creaking and the possibility of bug infestation common in old flooring.

Using wood throughout the house created a warm and enveloping feeling, but central heating can be very unkind to it. To

PORTE

Even if an Italian country farmhouse is in fairly good condition, it's likely that the ground floor was originally used as animal stalls. This means that at the very least some sort of new doors will be needed. Our house was in such bad shape that no doors could be salvaged (see page 160); we had to find old ones at salvage yards. In the house in the Maremma (see page 86), no doors existed at all, so new doors were commissioned. Some fine doors in the Da Sie house were reused; the home owners found antique doors to make up the balance (see page 72).

Interior doors, or *porte,* are fairly easy to find; they're usually coated with many layers of paint, which must be stripped. Exterior doors, or *portone,* are heavier, double-paneled affairs that often have wrought-iron locking mechanisms. They're more costly and slightly harder to find. Salvage yards and antiques dealers are good sources for both kinds; dealers may have a larger selection of fancier or older ones.

Installing antique doors usually calls for some modifications. Some can be mounted directly to the wall with iron hinges. Others require custom-built frames.

The three drawings below illustrate *portone,* or front entry doors: an interior face (left), and an interior face (center) with its exterior face (right). The doors are constructed using two thicknesses of wood, the planks placed vertically on the inside and horizontally on the outside. A grating above the door allows air and light to enter when the main door is closed.

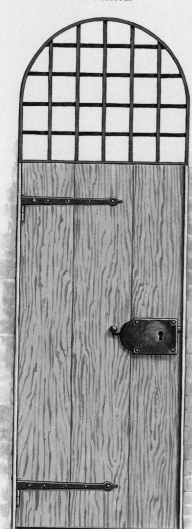

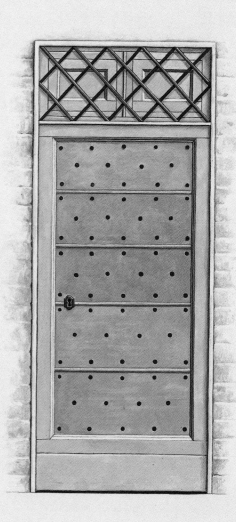

THE HOUSE IS THREE STORIES TALL: living room and kitchen are on the first floor, bedrooms on the second floor, and guest rooms on the third floor, left. A wrought-iron pergola off the kitchen, above, is covered with wisteria and roses. Handmade bricks pave the terrace and a walkway that surrounds the house.

combat its drying effects, all the wooden surfaces, from the highest beam to the floor planks, are treated every few years with a special mixture of wax and oil.

While it would have made more sense to have new doors and windows made, the Da Sies instead chose to preserve what they could of the originals. Whenever possible, the old fixtures were restored and reinstalled; when they were too far gone to be saved, they were replaced with elements from antiques shops and salvage yards. The home owners also chose to retain all of the door openings at their original scale, which made finding old doors to fit in all the more challenging. ■

TUSCANY

SATURNIA

IN ITALY, MOST RESTORATION

jobs start out with a romantic, if somewhat dilapi-

dated pile of moss-covered stones, rich with the

promise of recapturing centuries of history. But what

if a house's past is measured in decades rather than

centuries? And the nearest thing you have to weath-

ered bricks is reinforced concrete?

American writers David Leavitt and Mark

Mitchell had been living in Italy for four years, first

in Florence and then in Rome, when they decided

to move to the country, away from urban chaos.

They began looking for a house in Saturnia, a small

medieval town in the Maremma hills where they'd

been spending weekend escapes from the city. Known

for its thermal springs, the town and surrounding

countryside were off the beaten track for most tourists, both Italian and foreign.

Although the Maremma is the southernmost part of Tuscany, it's a far cry from the region with which most of us are familiar. I first visited the area more than twenty years ago on a drive inland from the coast. The road swerved gently over the hills, first passing through hazelnut groves but eventually giving way to the rougher landscape of the Maremma. Woods melted into fields populated by ghostly white steers and *butteri,* the cowboys who still herd them. We smelled our destination before we actually saw it: a warm sulfurous wind blew in the open windows of the car. We parked, tumbled out, and were soon sinking into the warm spring, which has made this spot a thermal attraction since Roman times. Warm water bubbles up and runs down over stones, and the pools at the bottom are lined in therapeutic mud.

Mark and David first considered buying a small place in the village of Saturnia itself, but eventually started looking at bigger places in the countryside. The only prerequisite was that the house be ready to move into, since the thought of embarking on a restoration

THE WINTER GARDEN, left, was originally an open porch used to store agricultural tools. The arches were glazed with steel-framed windows. Previous spread: The main change to the south side of the house was the addition of a small terrace off the study on the second floor. This was created using the landing from the original external staircase, which was eliminated. The space below houses the furnace. To achieve a weathered look on the exterior, pigments, including brick powder and yellow sand, were mixed into the plaster. The colors varied from batch to batch, giving the desired uneven effect.

IN THE STUDY looking out over the valley, French doors give on to a small terrace, above. Right: The home owners mixed the best of English style—comfortable chairs, plenty of bookshelves—with construction details that are purely Tuscan. The fireplace was created using salvaged stones. A smaller wood-burning stove in the fireplace opening is the owners' choice for an easy and economical way to heat the room. The banister on the new staircase and the curtain rods were handcrafted by a blacksmith in Rome.

SCALE

A self-supporting open staircase is constructed in much the same way as a traditional roof. Large oak or chestnut beams support smaller beams, which in turn are topped by a layer of terra-cotta tiles, visible between the beams from below. A layer of reinforced concrete is then topped by the stairs, in this case made of carved stone.

Almost without exception, the staircase or staircases in an Italian farmhouse were located on the outside of the house, providing access to the farmer's living quarters on the second floor. The first floor was reserved for livestock. The lack of a communicating internal staircase kept the two areas as separate as possible—an excellent idea for sanitary reasons!

The design of a new internal staircase is one of the most important, and difficult, aspects in a farmhouse restoration. A new staircase occupies a surprising amount of space—an area that seemed quite large as an entrance hall, for example, can be halved by its addition. An equally important consideration is locating the upper landing of the stairs in such a way as to give sensible access to all second-floor rooms.

The structure of the staircase can either be self-supporting and open, constructed in much the same way as a roof, with beams and tiles (see page 156). Or it can be closed, resting on masonry walls on the floor (see previous spread); the resulting space underneath is excellent for storage. Treads are usually made out of the same material as the floor. Terra-cotta tiles are often used, but they're thicker than floor tiles, since the edge of the step hangs out beyond the riser and is subjected to more stress. They're generally finished with a rough edge, in the same way as the floor tiles. If a less rustic look is desired, special tiles are available with finished rounded edges.

Other options for the treads include old stone steps salvaged from villas or urban palaces. Often extremely beautiful, they exist in a wide range of materials including travertine, *pietra serena*, marble, and local stone. Wood can also be used.

It's often possible to adapt the iron railing from the original external staircase. New railings and handrails, usually of forged iron, can be commissioned from a local metalsmith (see previous spread).

In most cases the original outside staircase is either eliminated or adapted for a new use. The upper level often becomes a terrace, while the lower volume is used for storage, accessible from either inside or out.

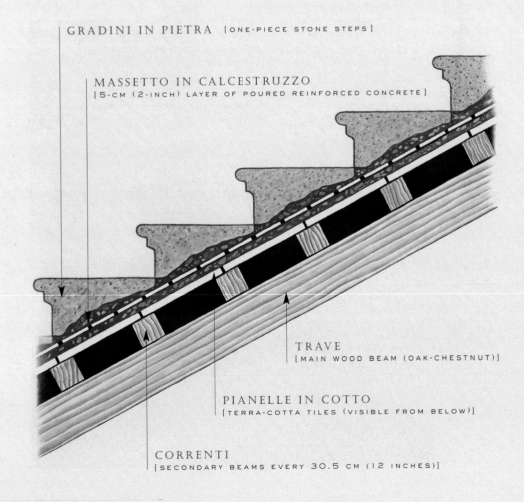

GRADINI IN PIETRA [ONE-PIECE STONE STEPS]

MASSETTO IN CALCESTRUZZO
[5-CM (2-INCH) LAYER OF POURED REINFORCED CONCRETE]

TRAVE
[MAIN WOOD BEAM (OAK-CHESTNUT)]

PIANELLE IN COTTO
[TERRA-COTTA TILES (VISIBLE FROM BELOW)]

CORRENTI
[SECONDARY BEAMS EVERY 30.5 CM (12 INCHES)]

was too daunting. That they finally decided on a ruin was the result of two months of fruitless searching; in this sparsely populated corner of Tuscany, suitable houses are few and far between. Their fears about tackling a restoration were eventually allayed by my husband, whom they trusted to see them through this complicated and very foreign architectural adventure.

The house they settled on, perched on a hill overlooking a pristine landscape, was one of many built in the 1950s and 1960s as part of a rural land reform project in the area. All the dwellings have identical blueprints: downstairs stalls for animals, and upstairs, reached by an external staircase, a few rooms to house a single family. This relatively modern building meant that the construction was still sound—steel beams and reinforced concrete ensured that the walls and roof were in good shape. In an old house, rotten beams and crumbling mortar usually mean that walls are easily knocked down. The solid construction of this house made it more economical to retain most of the existing structure, so almost all the internal divisions were left as they were. The one change was the addition of an internal staircase.

THE DINING ROOM, above right, and the kitchen, below right, are located on the ground floor in the space originally used as animal stalls. Since the building's internal divisions weren't changed, this meant that the smallish proportions of these rooms was a given. New windows were opened up in both rooms, not a simple task since the concrete construction was so solid. The kitchen cabinetry was custom-built in Rome; the countertop, of Carrara marble from a quarry in northern Tuscany, was cut locally by a craftsman who carves tombstones.

Yet for all its solidity, everyone felt that the house was a bit cold and that giving it warmth was the main objective. In an effort to avoid a feeling of false rusticity, the owners had all the windows and doors made to order and painted to achieve a clean, classic look. Handmade floor tiles were used throughout to warm up the spaces. New pine beams were installed on the downstairs ceiling and painted the same color as the walls and ceiling to lend movement and texture to the otherwise box-like rooms. Many of the decorative elements, including fabrics, paints, and even the kitchen sink, were found in London.

In the end, the home owners are glad they decided to restore a house rather than move into a "ready made." This allowed them to custom-build everything they could dream of. Both men are over six feet tall and find Italian kitchen countertops too low. One of their best memories is standing in the carpenter's workshop in the suburbs of Rome, pretending to cut carrots as the carpenter raised and lowered a countertop to suit their height. ■

FITTING IN CLOSETS is always a challenge in Italian farmhouses, since the original buildings had few or none. The solution in the master bedroom, above left, was to build floor-to-ceiling, double-level closets. The doors are glass-fronted and lined with fabric to give a light effect. The home owners, self-professed Anglophiles, chose wooden wainscoting for their very un-Italian master bath (left). The dark blue paint was actually imported from England (as were all the paints used in the house). Opposite: There is a magnificent view from every window, including all the villages—Saturnia, Montemerano, and Manciano—across the valley.

A HOUSE WITH A

COURTYARD

EVERYONE HAS A WAY OF measuring the place in which they live. Some people boast of the number of rooms they have. Others tell you how long it took them to build their home. Ferenc Maté, who, with his wife Candace, painstakingly oversaw the restoration of a Tuscan farmhouse, has a different measure stuck in his mind: the number 245. Every day for almost a year, he drove from his village to the construction site of their new home— 245 curves to get there, 245 curves to go back.

Granted, most of us wouldn't complain about the landscape he was "forced" to drive through. This tranquil corner of Tuscany is blessed with rolling hills planted with regiments of vineyards providing some of the best wine in Italy. The cycles of the vines define

the seasons. In the spring, fresh green buds appear on the seemingly dormant branches. By summer, entire valleys are a rich carpet of bright green leaves, with pea-size fruits just beginning to show through. Come September, the grapes have swelled and turned a deep purple, the bunches hanging heavy and ready to be hand-picked and begin the magical transformation into wine. My favorite time, though, is the fall, when the leaves turn a shockingly brilliant red for several weeks, before slowly falling to the ground. The vines are dormant until the cycle begins once again in the spring.

The Matés have had a similar love affair with the region. After first renting, then buying, a previously restored farmhouse, they eventually realized that what they really wanted was a place of their own to restore from scratch. Several things made the falling-down farmhouse they chose different from countless others they'd seen. The structure had lots of movement to it. It wasn't just one solid block; there were traces of at least

THE ENCLOSED courtyard is an original feature of the farmhouse, used to store farm equipment. Today it's a good place to grow delicate plants. Right: The arched openings leading to the house on three sides have been closed in by windows: the two large windows are part of the corridor on page 101, and the French doors lead to the kitchen. Previous spread: At least twelve different additions are reflected in the house's staggered roofline. Masons on the job wanted to hide the seams between the centuries, but the home owners insisted on retaining the building's history. Ancient olive trees were transplanted from nearby properties.

twelve different additions dating back at least six hundred years, and each had left its mark. They also fell in love with its courtyard, and especially with its location. Set on twenty-eight hectares, the house backed up to a wild wooded area but overlooked cultivated fields and magnificent vistas.

The building, however, proved to be deceptively solid looking. The walls were standing and most of the roof was still in place, but it soon became apparent that the mortar holding it all together had turned to little more than mud. A total renovation was in order. The decision was made to leave the floor plan as intact as possible. An internal staircase had to be constructed, windows had to be added to the ground floor, and the three dark rooms toward the front of the house—originally a warren of sheep stalls—were to be combined into a big open kitchen and dining room. It was Candace who made all the decisions concerning flow of space and who made sure that new window openings maintained the look of irregularity and unevenness of the existing windows.

Although they had a work crew of five, Ferenc acted as architect, surveyor, and site manager. His on-site presence was essential, since he found it almost impossible to plan the house on paper. Both he and Candace were skilled woodworkers, having already built their own boat. Often they helped plane and set in the wooden elements.

Finding the old materials that would give the house the right patina of age required a lot of travel and searching. Other home owners doing more modern renovations of their own were more than happy to unload old beams, doors, and tiles onto crazy foreigners. Beams were carefully chosen and placed. If they didn't look like they'd always been

THE NEW STAIRCASE, opposite, was constructed of handmade bricks for the risers and terra-cotta tiles for the treads. The entrance hall is paved in sixteenth-century square terra-cotta tiles, painstakingly collected from salvage yards across Tuscany. Above: The corridor connecting the kitchen and the living room is paved in the same tiles. A bright pink painted baseboard, trimmed in blue, echoes local custom.

THE LIVING ROOM, left, once a tool shed, retains its arched openings, now closed in by steel-framed glass windows. The large window looks onto the enclosed courtyard, and the smaller arch takes in a view of the garden. The turn-of-the-twentieth-century ceiling was constructed of vaults built with brick and steel beams, left exposed. Above: The newly built fireplace in the corner of the living room was made of terra-cotta tiles and bricks. A salvaged wooden beam serves as the lintel.

there, they were moved. Ferenc estimates that about 10 percent of the pieces they installed were subsequently taken down.

But it was always a struggle to get the workers to accept the idea of imperfection. Their inclination was to turn everything into the new and perfect. This happened every time the Matés proudly presented their vintage finds to the crew.

"That's a great beam for the fireplace," one mason would say.

CUCINE

The kitchen in an old Italian farmhouse was of course its most important room. It probably had the house's only fireplace and thus its only source of heat.

Although for most of us it's a romantic notion to retain the original kitchen, in reality it's often neither possible nor practical: the room was almost always on the second floor, which is generally turned over to bedrooms and bathrooms in the new design. Though there are some exceptions—the Pfefferkorn kitchen (see pages 112, 113), on the second story, is exactly as it was save for the addition of a two-burner cooktop set on a marble-topped table—most contemporary plans call for relocating the kitchen to the ground floor, where it's easily accessible to the living and dining rooms as well as to the outside. Then it's redesigned from scratch.

Since the old fireplaces were often the only source of heat in the whole house, they were usually shallow and large in order to reflect as much warmth as possible. As a result, though, they often filled the room with a smoky haze. Modern versions have a deeper hearth and a smaller opening. They may not throw off as much heat, but they're perfect for cooking and grilling, and they make a handsome focal point for any kitchen. Antique mantelpieces and old stonework for the surrounds can be found at salvage yards. Often the mantelpiece from the original kitchen can be reused.

In Italy it's common to create kitchen cabinetry by constructing a masonry framework and attaching wooden cabinet fronts. A more modern and efficient way is to have the cabinets made completely of wood and set in. This saves space (masonry walls are quite thick) and affords a very tight construction that's easy to keep clean (as well as free of bugs and small animals). The key is tracking down a knowledgeable, sophisticated carpenter; the search should probably start in a city, where craftsmen are more likely to have had experience doing this kind of specialized work.

An increasingly popular option is to purchase an entire kitchen from a European manufacturer, as the Brandolinis did (see pages 30–31). The cabinetry, built to order, is of very high quality and offers clean, contemporary lines that will accommodate almost all major appliances. Both refrigerators and dishwashers can completely disappear behind custom-built facades.

Regardless of the style of the room, a wide range of materials for countertops, backsplashes, and floors is available. Granite, marble, and terra-cotta add beautiful decorative elements to both rustic and high-tech settings and everything in between, and they're all available in glorious abundance in Italy. The Kosuth kitchen on pages 134–35 combines steel countertops with beveled white tiles on the walls. Karen Wolman's kitchen (pages 192–93) plays a lacquered wood countertop against glazed Mexican tiles on the backsplash. Our kitchen (page 157) is enlivened by old terra-cotta floor tiles and a checkerboard pattern of cream- and terra-cotta-colored tiles on both countertop and backsplash.

A chestnut door, crafted by a local carpenter and set into a brick surround, hides the built-in refrigerator in the Maté kitchen.

"You mean to be placed over the fire-place as a lintel?" Ferenc asked naively.

"No. In the fireplace. Let's burn it!"

In the end, the restoration was a revelation to the Matés. "You start out with old tiles covered in manure, or an old beam covered in mud," says Ferenc. "You have to look past the rot. It's always a surprise, and it always comes out better than you think." ■

THE FOCUS OF THE KITCHEN IS THE OPEN HEARTH, built at counter level and used almost year-round. A small wood-burning oven to the left is used to bake bread. A window was opened above the sink to let in light as well as to allow a view over the garden and across the vineyard.

THE DINING AREA OPENS out via French doors to the covered terrace, opposite. The outdoor dining area, above, once used as a storage shed for wood, is located several yards away from the house. The home owners hadn't considered using it until they cleaned it out and realized that it was the perfect place for al fresco meals. The beamed roof is supported by massive stone masonry columns, which frame the view of the vineyard.

SAN CASCIANO DEI BAGNI

MOST PEOPLE HAVE AN IDYLLIC

vision of what life is like in the Italian countryside.

They equate moving into a country home with a return

to a simpler way of life. But in the end they wind up

adding modern comforts to their tumble-down farm-

houses that most farmers never dreamed of.

Peter Pfefferkorn had no such illusions. He

truly wanted to live the simple life epitomized by

the rustic architecture and textures of the typical

farmhouse of central Italy. Once he found his home,

he vowed not to change a thing. More than twenty

years later, he has pretty much stuck to his original

plan, and walking into his home in San Casciano dei

Bagni is like stepping back in time.

This area of Tuscany has long attracted Italians in search of country homes. Cetona (where fashion designer Valentino has his retreat) is just over the hill, and San Casciano itself boasts well-known thermal springs. But two decades ago it had yet to attain its chic reputation. San Casciano was no more than a sleepy little hamlet where the action revolved around the one public phone in the central bar and the farmhouses were owned by locals who continued to work the land.

A COVERED PORCH ON THE GROUND FLOOR, opposite, is a typical part of farmhouses, used to park tractors and store equipment. The home owner restored the space, retaining all the original elements, and now uses it as the outdoor dining room and kitchen. He made the chestnut table in his woodworking shop, located at the other end of the house. Above: A two-burner cooktop, fueled by a canister of gas, is more than sufficient to brew the breakfast coffee al fresco each morning. A wooden plank, resting on beams that were already set into the stone wall, acts as a countertop. An original wood-burning oven is fired up on special occasions to roast such delicacies as lamb and potatoes. Previous spread: Some trees have died in the twenty years since the house was bought, but others have been planted to take their place, and numerous flowering bushes soften the rough edges of the old stone house.

Peter knew from the very beginning that he wanted to do all the necessary work with his own two hands. He took a two-month paid leave from his job in Berlin, laid down a mattress in the house, and began the renovation. His first task was stabilizing the roof and replacing rotted wooden beams and terra-cotta tiles.

For the next two summers he lived with no electricity, running water, or phone. Eventually water was brought to the house, and a toilet and bath were installed in the downstairs cow stall.

The house was furnished with used pieces—as the farmers in the area upgraded to more modern homes in town, Peter bought their furniture. Ironically, when he purchased the house, Peter wanted to live like the farmers, and now the farmers have moved on!

Today, floors still tilt and doors still creak. The walls are still mottled shades of pink, just as they were twenty years ago. Door and window frames balance precariously on

MOST FARMHOUSE restorations include a completely new kitchen. The owner chose to keep the original, with only a few concessions to modern comforts. Above left: An old wooden table is topped with a slab of stone and a two-burner cooktop. Below left: A breakfront, bought from neighbors, is big enough to hold the tableware. Two still lifes, painted by the home owner, flank the cabinet. Opposite: The large open hearth was the heart of the farmhouse kitchen. While it probably smokes and uses more wood than more modern, enclosed fireplaces, the owner didn't change a thing. It still boasts the iron hooks and chains that were used to hold pots of beans and stews to cook slowly over the embers.

original hinges, and only some of the glass has been replaced. "Nowadays people redo everything," says Peter, "but that's not me. I prefer things to remain as they are. I like imperfect things, and get nervous if something is too perfect. Things are much nicer if they have an old patina—like a worn Persian rug, colorful and intricate but with its history showing proudly."

That said, he does sometimes stray from his strict philosophy of the "don't touch/do-it-myself" rule. He recently had a pool put in by a contractor. ∎

THE MASTER BEDROOM, opposite, opens directly off the kitchen, where the massive fireplace supplies the house's only heat. Above right: The bathroom on the lowest level of the house can be reached only by walking outside and down the hill. The low doorway (the burlap protects those who forget to duck) leads to the toilet. For many years it was the only bathroom in the house. Bowing to convenience, the home owner recently installed a toilet and sink upstairs, off the kitchen.

A HOUSE WITH A LOGGIA NEAR

SIENA

THE ITALIAN WAY OF LIFE IS decidedly on the slow side. That's what attracts many foreigners to this country, including me. That said, the amount of waiting involved in restoring country farmhouses can try the patience of even the most relaxed Italian.

"Restoring this farmhouse was certainly a learning experience," says a fashion designer who commutes from Milan to her home outside Siena each weekend. "Perhaps my biggest lesson, however, was learning patience." She sought out a home in the area of Italy she considered to be real countryside: the Tuscan hillsides and valleys to the south of Siena. She spent months driving over hills punctuated by the sharp dark green forms of cypresses and ramshackle

farmhouses. The growing popularity of the region made the task all the more difficult. Bordering what is known as Chiantishire (for its strong appeal to the British), the central hills of Tuscany have been a vacation spot for foreigners for decades, and many of the farmhouses were snapped up and renovated long ago. The area is well known through films (think of Bertolucci's *Stealing Beauty* and Anthony Minghella's *The English Patient*) as well as the books of Frances Mayes (has anyone not read them?). When most people think of Italy, it's precisely this landscape they have in mind.

This house was in a lovely location, with just about perfect views. Soft hills changed with the seasons; fields of sunflowers, green shafts of wheat, rich red earth turned over to await the next cycle of planting. Windows framed a view of nearby Siena, its medieval spires glowing in the sunset.

The building itself was another matter. It was an unforgiving mass of a farmhouse with awkward proportions and little in terms of ornamentation. Still, the owner felt drawn to the building and the land. Enter Marco Vidotto, an architect from Siena, who came highly recommended by mutual friends. His first reaction was one of dismay, but when he looked deeper into the heart and soul of the building, he began to suspect that through the centuries an integral part of its original design had been ripped away. By examining the traditional architecture of the Sienese countryside, and making an almost archaeological inquiry into the house itself, he came to the conclusion that a double-story arched loggia originally had fronted the house and formed an imposing fulcrum for the structure.

Convincing the strict local building commission of this fact was more difficult.

THE LOWER LEVEL OF THE LOGGIA, opposite, which opens off the kitchen, serves as an outdoor living room, with a view of Siena framed by the brick arch. The low coffee table was designed by the owner and made by a local blacksmith of handmade terra-cotta tiles set into a wrought-iron frame. Above: The kitchen fireplace, with its massive hood, was designed by the architect. Open stone shelving holds baskets, plates, and serving dishes. Previous spread: The double-tiered loggia looks as though it has been there for centuries. In fact, it is a meticulous reconstruction of the original sixteenth-century design.

The architect was not only proposing changing the architectural character of the building (which is usually forbidden), he was, in theory, adding to the volume of the structure. Having been rebuffed by the commission on his first try, he warned the owner that she was in for a long wait—years, perhaps—until the necessary proof of the original house could be unearthed. In the meantime, work was begun on a smaller hayloft on the property, and the owner was able to move in within a year (albeit without running water,

THE SMALL STUDY ON THE GROUND FLOOR, above, is a medley of peach and terra-cotta tones. The high, narrow window—too high, really, to allow a view—is the original opening. "I wanted a house, not a reconstructed villa, so I tried to retain as many of the original elements as possible, even when they proved slightly inconvenient," says the owner. Right: The large living room takes up the entire east end of the ground floor. The modern fireplace is on the new wall that now divides this room from the adjacent kitchen.

ONE END OF THE LIVING ROOM, above, is dominated by a pair of large windows, formerly bricked over. Once the architect received permission to open them up, a local carpenter created the frames. Opposite, above: "One of the advantages of waiting for permits to arrive was that I had a great opportunity to get to know all the local artisans in the area," says the home owner. The windows, including these in the second-floor bedroom, were all handcrafted in wood by a carpenter in nearby Monteroni using traditional techniques. Opposite, below: Handmade terra-cotta tiles in a warm peach color set the tone for the entire decorating scheme. The owner hired artist Jackie Tune to study the light in each room and choose shades to apply in a mottled, uneven way on the walls, to echo the feel of the floor tiles. Following spread: The swimming pool is set at the edge of the property, away from the house, so as not to detract from the building's sculptural presence in the landscape.

electricity, or phone). At the same time, the architect went to work in the historical archives; he finally came up with the documentation to support his intuition: the house did in fact originally have a loggia. The building commission approved the plans.

Living on a construction site is an eye-opening experience. It takes courage to spend each day amid backhoes and masons. Yet there are advantages for those brave enough. When work finally began on the main house, the owner was able to follow every step from her roost in the hayloft.

Most people arrive ill prepared for a project of this scope, focusing on the superficial issues such as colors and textures rather than space flow and volume. Granted, it's difficult to imagine a kitchen or living room in place of pig troughs and cow stalls. When the architect wanted to block up an archway between two ground-floor rooms that would become the kitchen and the living room, he had the opening boarded over so the owner could better understand the new proportions of the two rooms.

When it came to color, the owner was intent on incorporating terra-cotta tones throughout the overall scheme. But newer tiles had become very red over the years; as the pits in Tuscany where the clay was traditionally mined went deeper and deeper, the iron content rose and the baked tiles took on a ruddier hue, very different from the peachy tiles in older houses. After much research, the owner found a manufacturer who mined clay in Umbria and made the light-colored tiles.

"Owning property changes you," the owner says. "You want it to live and breathe and survive, as it did for hundreds of years before you arrived. Although it's often a struggle, it's a beautiful one." ■

TERRACOTTA

Odd angles and corners in farmhouses make the paving pattern all the more important. Below, three rows of rectangular tiles form the border of a carpetlike pattern of square tiles set at an angle. A central square is formed by another three rows of rectangular tiles, creating the illusion of regular proportions.

It's a rare and lucky owner who is able to retain his home's original flooring, especially in an abandoned farmhouse. Peter Pfefferkorn kept his floor tiles (see page 108); they were in good condition, and he had no plans to install a new plumbing or heating system, which would have entailed running pipes underneath the tiles. Most houses, however, require more drastic intervention.

Once an old building is stabilized and new structural floors are built, the last layer is usually tile or wood. Occasionally, stone is used, especially on the ground floor, where the extra weight and thickness isn't a problem (see page 249). Traditionally, the living quarters of farmhouses in central Italy were paved with terra-cotta tiles (*cotto*), and this is what most people use today. One choice is using old tiles, as the Matés did (see pages 100–101). With salvage yards becoming more common, it's fairly easy, though not cheap (the tiles were originally cemented into the floor and are difficult to extract intact) to buy enough old tiles to pave an entire house. They come in various shapes and sizes, the most common being rectangular. The rarer square-shaped ones are even more sought after and therefore more costly.

Another type of old tiles are the rectangular terra-cotta *mezzane*. Because they were never grouted, they are easily salvaged from old buildings and are therefore comparatively inexpensive. An honest dealer will tell you if his merchandise is roof or floor tiles, but in any case, *mezzane* have several obvious characteristics. They're usually partly painted on one side, with only the portion where the beam crossed remaining unpainted. And they're rougher and more porous on both sides than floor tiles, which are worn down on the side that was exposed to foot traffic.

When buying old tiles, it's important that those in every batch—for each room at least—be exactly the same size. Seemingly similar tiles can vary by as much as a centimeter (half an inch); even half a centimeter can cause installation problems entailing an enormous amount of unsightly grouting.

The best-quality new terra-cotta tiles come from Tuscany. This *cotto toscano* is made from a very high-quality clay, which dries hard and is extremely resistant to wear and tear. The finished look is very regular, the color a deep red. Handmade tiles are a less industrial-looking choice if you're buying new. Excellent ones come from a small town in Umbria called Castelviscardo, near Orvieto; they have a rough texture similar to old tiles and their color is warm and yellow, lighter than those from Tuscany. All handmade tiles have to be ordered well in advance, since

they're left to dry in the open, and in some places still baked in wood-fueled kilns.

The advantage of new tiles, whether handmade or industrial, is that they can be installed with tile glue, since they're all of a consistent size and thickness. This saves money in terms of both labor and drying time. Because old tiles vary so much in size and thickness, they must be installed with traditional mortar. This takes up space, costs more in terms of labor, and involves longer drying time (water-based mortar can take weeks to months, depending on the season).

Herringbone patterns can be set at right angles or at a diagonal to the wall. A rule of thumb is that diagonally placed tiles require more cuts to fit into the scheme, thus involving more waste and labor and increasing the cost of installation.

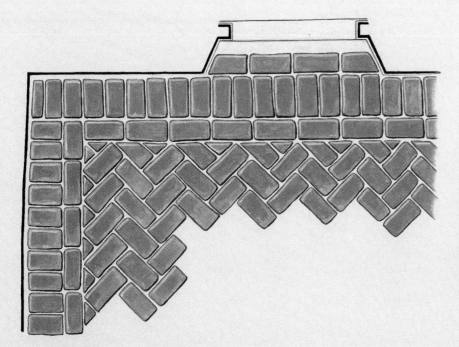

A HILLSIDE HOUSE IN
SAN CASCIANO DEI BAGNI

PROVIDENCE OFTEN BRINGS us to places we would never have imagined. When I was growing up in St. Louis, I could hardly have guessed I would one day be raising my family in ancient Rome and the hills of Umbria. In a similar way, American artist Joseph Kosuth let fate take him by the hand thirty years ago and found himself the owner of a farmhouse in the small Tuscan town of San Casciano dei Bagni. The only change he made to turn the dwelling into a more habitable one was to bring in running water and install a bathroom. There was no electricity and no heating system save for the fireplace; after the sun set, he was forced to work by candlelight. When the weather turned colder, he

THE LIVING ROOM FORMS THE NUCLEUS of the upper floor, above and opposite. The large space was the kitchen of the old farmhouse, and the open fireplace was salvaged from that room. Two doors on the wall behind the sofa led to a room that used to house water cisterns and now serves as a studio. One of the doorways was walled up, and the resulting niche was converted into bookshelves. Previous spread: The external staircase was eliminated and the upper landing converted into a covered terrace accessible from the second-floor living room. The space below the stairs, on the ground floor, is used to house the boiler for the newly installed heating system.

would place buckets of hot coals under his desk to warm his feet.

In typical Italian fashion, it took several years before he was able to run in a phone line, but electricity still remained a dream. He ended up installing a fax machine to run on a special small generator. There he was, receiving faxes—and reading them by candlelight! It was all very romantic, including trips to the local thermal springs for hot baths. Finally, though, he decided that perhaps life was a little too rustic for his growing

family—his wife, Cornelia Lauf, and their two daughters. The place was charming, but waking up with chunks of plaster in their beds decidedly was not.

The Kosuths turned to my husband, Domenico, for help in reining in the dangerous aspects of the structure. Unfortunately, once he inspected the house, Domenico found that a whole wall had become detached from the rest of the building and was slowly making its way down the hill, taking the roof with it. It was just a matter of time before the whole thing collapsed.

The floor plan and heating and electrical systems also needed some readjusting. Two

A NEW SET OF INTERNAL STAIRS leads from the kitchen to the upper landing, above. Right: Rather than use pseudo-rustic materials such as handpainted tiles, the home owners chose thoroughly modern solutions that contrast nicely with the exposed stones of the original walls. Beveled white Belgian tiles from the 1930s cover the walls, and stainless steel forms the countertop.

IN THE NEW SECOND-FLOOR BATHROOM, almost all of the antique fixtures—including the tub, sinks, and facucets—were found in Belgium, where the home owners had been living. Opposite: The French doors in the master bedroom used to lead to a small balcony connected to the landing of the external stairs. When the stairs and balcony were eliminated, a wrought-iron railing was installed.

small children made the fact that the bedrooms were upstairs, the only bathroom downstairs, and the staircase external even more inconvenient; the charms of tromping down stone stairs in the middle of the night only carries so far. And heating and insulation had to be added so the house could be used year-round.

To begin with, the foundations and subfoundations had to be stabilized without dismantling the entire house (see page 139). Next, space had to be carved out for a new internal staircase without disrupting the flow of the existing rooms. Finally, new bathrooms and a boiler room had to be created.

Like many foreign home owners, the Kosuths had a romantic, almost religious attachment to every brick and stone in the house, so they found it very upsetting to see things such as the external staircase torn apart and used in different places in the house. The Italian lack of appreciation for the old—Italians have, after all, lived with this load of history all their lives—led the couple to look outside Italy when choosing fixtures for their bathrooms. They found vintage tubs, sinks, and even faucets in Belgium. (Oddly enough, although Europe is on the metric system, the plumbing fixtures are all measured in inches, so a showerhead from the United States or England will easily fit into the Italian plumbing system.)

When it came to the heating system, though, the couple decided to be thoroughly modern and use solar power. Panels installed on the roof supply hot water in the bathrooms and kitchen year-round. During the winter, when the house is empty except on weekends, the system is switched over to run warm water through radiant heating pipes in the floor. Although the power isn't enough to heat the house on its own, it maintains a constant

tepid temperature that allows the building to be heated quickly by a gas-fueled heater when the family arrives on Friday evening.

Unfortunately, the inroads of modernization are changing the look and feel of these farmhouses forever. The last generation that actually grew up with and lived in these types of houses—people who remember which room was used for drying prosciutto and where water was found—is all disappearing, and with it much of the history of these places will be gone. ∎

A COVERED PORCH OPENS off the ground-floor living room and overlooks the man-made lake below. When the owners bought the house, there was a marshy area at the bottom of the valley. One summer they arrived to find that a dike had been built, and a lake, perfectly situated to accommodate their view, had suddenly appeared.

FONDAZIONI

Foundations of old farmhouses are usually no more complicated than a slight widening of the wall below-ground. To reinforce and stabilize existing foundations, micropiles (*micro pali*) are used.

Restoration always comes with surprises. Some are good, like the discovery of a bit of fresco painting or an ancient carved stone lintel. Others can be disconcerting, like finding that the mortar holding the stones together is no more than dust. One thing that's almost impossible to ascertain before construction begins is the state of the foundation.

It's not uncommon to find farmhouses that were built around the nucleus of an old watchtower, but more likely the house has humbler origins. Country farmhouses are by definition poor buildings and often have rough or nonexistent substructures, with the stone walls being set only a foot or less into the ground. And since many of these buildings have long been abandoned, the lower portions of the walls have eroded, creating structural damage.

There are various ways to reinforce foundations. One way is to build a buttress, a traditional method requiring the construction of a massive sloping wall. A more technically advanced solution is to use a system called *micro pali*, or micropiles, in which a specialized machine digs deep cylindrical holes in the ground along the base of the existing wall, on the interior as well as the exterior side. Then a cylindrical steel cage is lowered into each hole and filled with pressurized concrete. The inner and outer rows of cement-filled holes are then connected with steel and concrete, which creates an extremely strong structure that will stop any ground shifts or sinking of the existing wall. This is the method that was used in the Kosuth house.

A third method requires creating a new subfoundation, used when the existing floor level is lowered so far that the foundations disappear. In this case, the contractor digs below ground level and builds a new stone wall, piece by piece, underneath the existing one.

A WATCHTOWER IN
LATTAIA

THE AREA SOUTH OF TUSCANY around Massa Marittima is blessedly off the beaten track. It's not "on the way" to anywhere, and few cultural monuments attract busloads of tourists. The Upper Maremma's hills are rugged and don't give way to vineyards until you go east toward Montalcino. And you have to head west to reach the more populated Tuscan coastline. The inland landscape retains a tranquility and timelessness that isn't always easy to find in the region these days.

The small village of Lattaia is located not far from Roccastrada, and not near much else. When Daniele Cariani and Gianni Cacciarini first saw their small crumbling house on the edge of this medieval village, they were attracted to the simplicity of the

structure. They decided that it met their minimal requirements—a roof, doors, staircase, and an adequate number of rooms. Views from the west-facing windows took in the entire plain below and even the sea, a half-hour drive away.

But it was the romanticism of nature that finally convinced the couple that this was the place they had been looking for. When

WHILE CLEARING OUT THE BASEMENT, left, the home owners came across large boulders that may date from the original ninth-century foundations of the watchtower. Olive oil and wine are stored in the naturally cool and dark room. The sculpture is a plaster cast of a classical statue depicting the goddess Diana. Above: The original pig stalls, made out of bricks and having wooden doors, were cleaned up and painted and are now used for art exhibitions. Since the stalls hadn't been used in decades, there was no animal odor to eliminate. French doors, painted green, lead to the garden. Previous spread: Bushes of Rosa Ballerina burst into bloom each June at the base of the old tower.

THE GARDEN LIVING ROOM, above, is located at one end of the old animal stalls on the ground floor. The sculptural, double-sided fireplace was designed by one of the home owners. Opposite, above: The landing on the second floor leads to a small hallway paved in the original terra-cotta tiles; it's divided from the guest room by a partition made of wood so as not to put additional stress on the foundation. The doorway at the end of the hall leads to the guest bathroom. A sunny yellow 30-centimeter-wide (15-inch) baseboard runs along all the walls on this level. Opposite, below: The upstairs living room, with its low beamed ceilings and fireplace, is used all winter. Here, and throughout the house, the window frames and inner shutters are painted a vivid shade of green.

they stepped into the garden, they were overwhelmed by the sight of an ancient apple tree in full flower. The branches were laden with heavenly scented blossoms, and the petals on the ground reminded the men of a Japanese painting. In this sweet setting, they were able to overlook the fact that the building was surrounded by a virtual junkyard inhabited by several snakes.

The house, situated at the edge of the village, dates to the tenth century. Because of its panoramic position, there is no doubt that it was a watchtower for the town. In fact, while clearing out the *cantina,* an arched space half submerged underground, workmen unearthed giant boulders that most likely formed the tower's foundation.

Daniele, a Florence-based architect, was sure of his design objectives. He wanted the house to be what it was when they found it, not some architect's version of it. The main order of business was stabilizing the existing structure; modern additions would gradually come later, and be done with a light hand.

Most of the ground floor had originally been a pigsty—literally. The small cubicles that had been the stalls, were left intact. Both Daniele and Gianni, a painter, use the space to host exhibitions. A large open area at one end of the floor was converted into a summer living room, which gives directly onto the garden. The bedrooms, dining room, kitchen, and winter living room are on the second floor.

The decor is eclectic, mainly because this is a second home for both owners, full of the furniture and objects that couldn't fit into their primary homes. The walls are a deep jade ("*verde maremma*") throughout, a color that carries the green of the garden into every room, even in the kitchen.

If the interventions inside the house were kept to a minimum, the garden has been created almost from scratch. After recovering from his infatuation with the flowering apple tree, Daniele realized that the town had been using the land as a dumping ground. As the men began to rip out the weeds and cart away the junk, they found a number of sturdy survivors from what must once have been a country garden. There were several other fruit trees, including a grand old fig, and grapevines bearing clusters of *uva fragola* wound their way up ancient olive trees.

With no experience designing gardens, Daniele immersed himself in all the books he could find and began visiting nurseries as well as other gardens. He spent ten years working on the grounds. Today, jasmine and more than fifty kinds of roses scent the air, and the large lawn gives way to flowering oleander and broom. The shrubs lead to the olive grove, making the transition from garden to farmland almost invisible. ■

THE FURNISHINGS IN the master bedroom, opposite, are mostly Tuscan flea-market finds. The doorway leads out to a small terrace overlooking the garden. Above right: An especially overgrown corner of the garden is perfect for cultivating shade-loving plants. Below right: A small enclosed terrace was created in the space just outside the pigsty. Seafoam and Iceberg roses, two of more than fifty types of roses grown here, bloom throughout the summer. The two beams that stick out from the wall, now painted green, most likely were used to support grapevines.

PISCINE

If the Cariani-Cacciarini swimming pool (left) looks slightly rustic, there's good reason. Because their village building commission decided that swimming pools have no place in the rugged and mostly agricultural landscape, the two home owners received permission to restore a former *bevitoia,* or drinking trough, for farm animals and turn it into a holding tank! A fountainhead sprays water into the pool several times a day, keeping things moving and doing away with the need for any kind of traditional pump. Every so often algacide is added; even so, the owners say they've gotten used to swimming with frogs.

Although most towns aren't as strict as Roccastrada, in some places it has become virtually impossible to build pools. As more people discover the joys of transforming farmhouses into vacation homes, the number of swimming pool requests has risen sharply. Fearing a blight of shimmering turquoise intrusions on the rural landscape, local boards have begun to refuse requests. The area known as the Argentario, a peninsula on the southern Tuscan coast—sometimes referred to as the East Hampton of Rome—is notoriously difficult. Yet even here, canny builders get around the restrictions by constructing "holding tanks for fire-fighting emergencies."

In areas where permission to build is more easily obtained, some building commissions have become more particular about the way the finished pool will look. This can mean integrating the pool into the surrounding landscape by choosing an appropriate color, or by using plantings to provide privacy while shielding the pool from view.

Once permission is granted, there are two choices in terms of construction. A prefabricated pool with a vinyl liner is a popular option—and generally the contractor's first choice, as it's the cheapest, fastest, and least problematic for him (see pages 126–27). Shapes and finishes are limited; many of the stock colors tend toward turquoise, though a darker color can always be special-ordered.

The other option is to build a pool out of poured reinforced concrete (see pages 162–63). Once the hole is dug, a frame of steel rebars is prepared and a wooden frame constructed to act as a form for the concrete. Almost anything can be applied to line the pool, from specially mixed epoxy paints and and colored plaster to mosaic, marble, or even terra-cotta tiles. Choices of shape, size, color, and finish are almost unlimited.

Italian summers are very hot, and a swimming pool provides welcome relief, but the climate during the remaining seven or eight months of the year means the pool won't be in use. Fuel costs usually preclude heating it, and electricity costs favor turning off the pumps for the winter. This means using a tarp covering, which isn't a pretty sight, so locating the pool so that it's not directly visible from the house is an important consideration if the house is to be used throughout the year. And while safety is always an issue, Italian law doesn't require pools to be fenced in.

U M B R I A

TODI

EVEN THOUGH BOTH DOMENICO

and I had experience in restoring houses in Italy—

he designing them, I writing about them—my real

education came through the odyssey of finding our

own pile of rubble and turning it into the home it is

today. Domenico had been working on renovation

projects in Umbria for several years, and each summer

we'd rent a house around Todi. We grew to love the

countryside and the people there, but a restricted bud-

get and the growing popularity of the area made

finding the right place to buy seem near impossible.

We followed every lead. Once, a carpenter

led us to an isolated, crumbling tower that seemed

perfect—until we discovered it overlooked a very

pungent pig farm. Another farmhouse slipped through

our fingers at a public auction. Then, one day, as we were having a cappuccino at a local bar, the postman asked why we looked so sad. When we told him how pessimistic we were about finding a ruin to restore, he said he knew just the place: "the house of Tomasso."

We wound up at what seemed like a dead end in a sunflower field. A farmer was kind enough to lead us, with me puffing and panting—I was eight and a half months pregnant with our first child—up a steep hill to a vine-covered stone farmhouse, seemingly untouched for decades. Although obviously derelict and abandoned to the elements, the

THE LIVING ROOM, opposite, off the dining room, has very low exposed-beam ceilings to create a cozy atmosphere. The base of the fireplace is an old paving stone from the Todi town square, and the mantelpiece came from an antiques dealer in the Marches. The sitting area at the other end of the room, above, with a sleep sofa, doubles as a guest room. Here, as in the rest of the house, the windows incorporate large single panes of glass, to frame uninterrupted views. Previous spread: Although our house was a complete ruin, we tried to minimize changes to the original external floor plan. We added the covered terrace off the second-floor bedroom, and used the two levels below to create bathrooms off the living room and guest suite. We also built the overhanging brick addition above the entrance door; this small space houses the shower and bathtub in the master bath.

weathered stones and rickety beams still held some promise. But it was when we turned our backs to this romantic heap that we were sold. The view was breathtaking: cultivated fields alternated with woods, vineyards popping up in between. There was even a crenellated castle on the next ridge, with a row of cypresses marching across the horizon. We knew we had found paradise.

By this time, we also knew exactly what we wanted the house to be and what the renovation pitfalls were. As a result, the work went surprisingly smoothly and amazingly fast—a mere nine months passed between the first scrape of the backhoe and our first night under our new roof.

The house—a farmhouse, parts of which date back two or three centuries—was, like many in the area, built for two families. Two outdoor staircases led to two separate apartments on the second floor; the ground floor had been reserved for the animals. Hacking our way through the vines that covered the building, we discovered yet another, semi-underground level below the stables.

THE DINING ROOM, above left, is used mostly for special occasions during the winter. The exposed stone walls are a dramatic touch. A new staircase, below left, leads from the dining room to the second floor. The fresco is a bit of whimsy that artist Matthew Imperiale created with acrylic paints after an Etruscan design. Opposite: Matte porcelain and terra-cotta tiles form a checkerboard pattern for the kitchen backsplash and countertop. Old chestnut beams supports the arch separating the cooking and eating areas. The window above the kitchen sink, opposite, looks out over the back of the house and my vegetable garden.

Over the years, the house had been almost overtaken by the woods surrounding it. While we loved the feeling of protection the trees created, glimpses of the view out over the valley were tantalizing, and we wanted to be able to watch the sun set over the hills. We began to slowly thin the trees toward the front of the house, being careful to spare two of the most splendid features of the property, an ancient walnut tree and an immense elm standing at least six feet over the roofline.

Most of the house's external walls were intact, but there wasn't much else to define it as a potential home. The roof was, for all intents and purposes, gone. This meant that the elements had done their damage: supporting interior beams had rotted away, causing the floors and tiles to crash to the ground. Doors and windows had similarly disappeared. Even deciding on a floor plan was a leap in the dark, since many of the spaces—including what was to become the ground-floor guest suite, the living room, and our bedroom—were entirely inaccessible because of the dilapidated condition of the building.

As our contractor repeated innumerable times, it would have been much easier to tear the place down and build from scratch, but we wanted to hold on to as much of the old structure as we could, even if it meant altering our plans if we came across a buttress that needed shoring up or a doorway that needed to be closed.

As foundations were dug and walls rebuilt, we began to search out additional architectural elements. Domenico purchased fourteen sets of antique doors from a dealer in the Marches, and the stone manatelpieces in the kitchen and the living room came from an old man in the same region who had salvaged them from abandoned farmhouses.

THE GUEST SUITE on the ground floor, above and opposite, has its own separate entrance. The room was collapsed when we first saw the house; the ceiling, which is now the floor of the living room above, had completely fallen in. Domenico designed the romantic canopy bed; it was constructed by a carpenter in Rome, then hung with embroidered linen panels. Two overstuffed armchairs make a comfortable little seating area in the room.

Our contractor managed to nab some old discarded paving stones from the main piazza in Todi, which we used to create steps leading from the dining room to the living room.

We used handmade terra-cotta tiles throughout the ground floor. Rather than wax them to a shiny finish, as is the norm in Italy, we left them in their rough, matte state. Upstairs, on the bedroom level, we decided to use wood instead of tiles for the floors, an unusual choice in Italian country homes if for no other reason other than age-old tradition. We were lucky enough to have a friend who had cut down several cypress trees a decade before. The wood, beautifully seasoned by the time we got to it, was cut into uneven lengths and widths and hand-installed. Its fragrant scent was an added bonus we hadn't expected, and all these years later it still fills the house with its perfume.

One of our most important design decisions was, in fact, a bit of an experiment. Domenico had always wanted to incorporate pigment directly into the final coat of plaster rather than simply painting the walls after the plaster was up. He thought this would give an added layer of texture to the rooms and make the colors appear to be part of the fabric of the walls. The contractor, who had never done this before, was hesitant to try, but soon he was grinding terra-cotta and mixing it into batches of plaster with raw pigments that Domenico had brought up from Rome. The result was splendid. Each room has slightly different warm earth tones, which seem to glow on their own and give the house the cozy feeling everyone remarks on.

Cooking is a large part of my life, and I knew from the very beginning that the kitchen would be the most important room in the house. The original one had been on

THE LARGE WINDOW IN THE MASTER BEDROOM, above, was a new addition that allows a breathtaking view of the valley. The wood beams were left unpainted; the rest of the ceiling was painted to match the walls. Opposite, above and below: In the master bathroom, a pair of sinks faces each other and forms a passageway to the shower. Handmade terra-cotta tiles pave the room, and hand-painted tiles from Vietri form a border around the tub and shower. Two antique doors lead to walk-in closets.

the upper floor, but keeping it there would have put it right next to the bedrooms. Instead, we knocked down a wall between two small stables on the ground floor to create one large space that would serve as both working kitchen and eating area. This enabled us to include almost all of the things I had ever dreamed of. The working part revolves around a central island, which separates the two areas. This oak-topped piece of furniture, designed by Domenico, incorporates a bookshelf and a spice rack as well as two deep rolling drawers for pots. What can't fit in the drawers hangs from a rack directly above. The double ovens are under a window that overlooks the garden so I can keep an eye on the kids while I'm cooking. The dishwasher and a large refrigerator are hidden in custom-made cabinetry.

But for all my kitchen's modern conveniences, my favorite part is the large open hearth. Although it looks as if it had been there since time began, it was actually designed by Domenico; it incorporates an antique lintel as well as old paving stones from the piazza in nearby Todi. Throughout the winter months, we never let the fire go out. ∎

THE SWIMMING POOL, right, is located on the old *àia*, or threshing ground. It's far enough away from the house so that in winter the covered pool doesn't become an eyesore, yet close enough for easy access. It also provides some of the best views from our property. The reinforced concrete was painted a dark gray to mimic a natural pond.

PREVENTIVI

The amount you paid for your new property may seem huge, but it's almost invariably surpassed by the amount you spend to actually fix the place up—even if it *looks* habitable and seems solid.

Once you've bought the house, you'll have to pay a notary's fee (see page 35), which amounts to 2.5 percent of the declared value of the property. (Most notaries charge a minimum fee of L.2.000.000, but since this varies, you should shop around.) If you used a real estate agent, you'll have to pay anywhere from 3 to 10 percent of the real (not the officially registered) sale price. Again, fees vary depending on the size of the property and the location of the agent.

You'll also have to pay a registration tax (Tassa di Registro) on the officially declared value—10 percent for properties that are "urban" and 17 percent for "rural." (Most houses are now considered urban, and if they aren't registered as such, they can be before the sale.) If the house is a primary residence—which must be declared and proven within a year of the purchase—the registration tax drops to 4 percent. But if the property being sold is owned by a registered company rather than an individual, there is a sales tax called I.V.A. (Imposta Valore Aggiunto, or Value Added Tax) of 20 percent of the declared value. Most construction estimates won't include this tax—often a surprise, especially to foreigners from countries where sales tax isn't usually added to services. In Italy, the contractor submits a monthly bill for work completed, plus a 20 percent tax.

An unofficial word about "official" prices: this is Italy, and some rules are made to be avoided or ignored. Many real estate agents say that Italian law works on the assumption that when a property is sold, the vendor will declare only about half of the actual value—hence the high rates of taxation. Official checks are exchanged in the notary's office; later, undeclared cashier's checks or cash are exchanged to make up the difference. While this may be accepted practice in certain parts of the country, it's still breaking the law.

If you've hired an architect, he or she will charge a fee governed by the official association of Italian architects, usually 8 to 16 percent of the overall construction cost. He'll probably gather bids from several contractors; the one you and he ultimately choose will then present an estimate, or *preventivo*, based on the architect's list of works. This usually includes only major construction work; he'll get separate estimates from the plumber, electrician, painter, carpenter, pool contractor, and other subcontractors the job calls for.

Estimates for the restoration and renovation of an old house are just that—estimates. Unlike building a new house, where every detail can be measured and precisely planned, restoring an old ruin presents a much different picture. There's often no strict plan to follow through the project. This is one of the most perplexing and scary parts of renovating a house in Italy, especially for foreigners. When we began work on our own home, we of course started out with a budget. We knew we'd have to be somewhat flexible;

One of the unforeseen items in our construction budget was the need for a new buttress. Built at the corner of the stone wall where one of the external staircases used to be, it was added to shore up the two existing walls.

what we didn't know is that we'd have to construct a massive buttress to hold up the south side of the house. And since three rooms were inaccessible, we had no way of knowing if the huge beams would have to be replaced. At the same time, we didn't hand over a blank check. We couldn't know exactly how many beams would have to be replaced, but since an estimate provides specific prices per square or linear foot of work, we did know how much they would cost per foot, installed. Nonetheless, construction budgets on restorations tend to balloon at an alarming rate. To avoid ugly surprises, a good rule of thumb is to tack on at least 20 percent to any estimate you receive.

SPOLETO

A TRANSPLANTED AMERICAN like me, Pam Moskow didn't really plan to live her life in Italy. But love decided her fate, as it did mine: she married an Italian, Franco Piersanti, and adopted his country as her own.

When Pam and Franco decided to bring a tumbledown building in an Umbrian village back to life, in no way did they imagine that they would be instrumental in keeping the spirit of the village alive as well. They first discovered the hills around Spoleto when Franco, a composer, was working on a production for the Spoleto Arts Festival. Rather than camp out at a hotel, they found a small cottage to rent for the summer—and ended up staying for nine years. But they kept dreaming of owning their own place. They

looked at a wide range of properties over the years and eventually realized they wanted to be in a village rather than isolated in the countryside.

Pam considers it fate that they finally wound up where they did. Although the house is in a small village, it's a freestanding building, and even has a bit of land in back for a garden. And it wasn't a complete ruin.

During the first weeks of reconstruction, Pam worked alongside the masons, chipping away at plaster and stones, trying to discover what elements were worth saving. Much to the dismay of many of their architect friends, she decided to keep almost everything exactly as it was. While she could have enlarged many of the rooms and perhaps altered the floor plan to make it flow more smoothly, she opted instead to preserve what she felt was the inherent poetry of the place.

Luckily, there was much to preserve. Unlike the residents of many small villages in Italy, which have allowed haphazard modernization, those of Poreta have always had an overriding sense of preservation and respect for their small town. Neither corrugated steel awnings nor reinforced concrete additions blemish the buildings. Pam and Franco's house was pretty much the way it had been for about two hundred years.

THE GROUND-FLOOR living room used to be the kitchen, complete with the huge fireplace and bread oven. Almost all of the furniture and most of the decorative objects come from flea markets. Previous spread: The home owners were lucky to find a freestanding house within a small village. They built a low stone wall to separate their "front yard" from the road.

Like many small villages in Umbria, Poreta was built up over the centuries around a fortress. The foundations of the house probably date back to the sixteenth century, when the Castello di Poreta was built on the hill above. The village grew according to the castle's fortunes. In 1703, after a large earthquake that brought down much of the castle, the residents used the loose bricks and stones to expand their own houses below. Local lore as well as archival documents indicate that Pam and Franco's house was once much bigger, taking up half the village. The balanced

THE DINING ROOM, ONCE THE PIGSTY, left, is now connected to the former pantry, which has been turned into the kitchen. Original niches near the ceiling hold some of the home owner's many flea-market finds. The staircase, above left, is in the sixteenth-century loggia, which had been closed in the nineteenth century. The stone sink, above right, was part of the old pantry. The home owner bought the Sicilian majolica tiles many years before she purchased the house.

and symmetrical facade was a double-tiered arched loggia housing a staircase. These arches were at some point closed in, and the house as it exists today is essentially the bricked-in loggia of the original *villa padronale*.

The only structural change made in the current restoration was to connect the ground-floor pigsty to the pantry, turning the resulting larger space into the dining room. Most of the floors still bear terra-cotta tiles, dating most likely to the eighteenth century. The large living room fireplace was the centerpiece of the old kitchen.

Neighbors had alerted Pam to the possibility that there were frescoes somewhere in the house. She spent months using special solvents to wipe away the layers of paint. Eventually she found two rustic painted birds, probably done by a farmer at the turn of the last century.

One of the things that Pam has given back to her village is the restoration of the ruined castle that used to be the center of village life. Sharing her neighbor's despair that there was little to keep the youngest generation from moving away to find jobs, she helped organize public fund raisers to turn the Castello into a thriving hotel and restaurant. Today it employs many of the town's youth. ■

" W E K E P T I T very clean and spare," says Pam of the bedroom, left. "It's the only room where our passion for flea-market discoveries doesn't intrude." The floor is wide planks of pine. A mobile made by Franco hangs from the ceiling. The master bath, above and below right, is large enough for an antique easy chair and bookshelves. The sink is set into the corner and surrounded by white tiles. Period mirrors are practical as well as beautiful.

ONE OF THE BIG SELLING POINTS of this house in town was the small garden. A small stone sink is lined with turquoise tiles found in a trash bin behind a bathroom supply shop. Landscape architect Sophy Roberts turned the area into a low-maintenance yet elegantly refined garden. Gravel paths take the pain out of watering too much lawn, which is limited to two small parterres in the classical plan.

Mercati e Fiere

Although many Italians now buy their furniture ready-made, there's a strong tradition to commission custom pieces. This practice stretches back centuries, and the most vivid illustrations of it are the antiques fairs staged monthly throughout the country, offering handcrafted furnishings dating from the thirteenth century to yesterday. Otherwise sleepy medieval towns are transformed into bustling commercial markets; Arezzo, Cortona, and Lucca in Tuscany are perhaps the best known. Dealers set up their stands, usually in the town's main piazza, on Friday evening; the sheer number of stalls can seem overwhelming. The cognoscenti know that all the best pieces are snapped up well before Saturday-morning cappuccinos, so the best bet is to hit the streets around dawn. Many visit regularly, even during the dead of winter when the wind whipping through the piazza makes frequent stops for caffè laced with a shot of brandy obligatory.

The fairs are often good places to hunt for large-scale architectural elements such as iron gates, marble fireplaces, and columns. Others offer temptingly disorderly assortments of tiles, urns, and other outdoor and garden pieces. Although the permanent antiques stores in major cities may consistently sell the more important and expensive items, it's the itinerant stands in the markets that offer the most surprises—and the eternal promise of unearthing a "find."

Although many stands offer true antiques, some mix the real with the faux. Dealers sometimes fashion new pieces such as tables and shelves from old wood salvaged from furniture too dilapidated to restore. Others offer brightly painted pieces inspired by eighteenth-century northern Italian fur-

An ornate seventeenth-century chair, stripped to reveal its original colors, was found at a flea market, as was the bedframe, which was fashioned from an old gate from the Dolomites, in northern Italy. The new sink is surrounded by hand-painted tiles from Portugal.

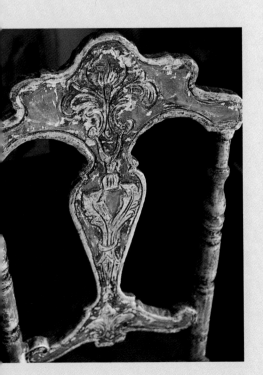

niture. When buying any antique, you should keep your eyes wide open and not be afraid to ask questions. If you like a piece and the price seems right, go ahead and buy it; don't worry about its pedigree or lack of one. And don't be afraid to bargain—it's accepted, and expected, behavior.

One of the thrills of frequenting the fairs is finding objects with lives beyond their intended original use. A nineteenth-century bit of wrought iron might make a beautiful sconce.

With the surge in country home restoration in the last ten years, more and more salvage yards have opened. Often located on the outskirts of small towns, they're a great source of architectural objects and materials from a range of periods. Terra-cotta tiles for both floors and roofs, dismantled stone fireplaces, stone lintels and portals, wooden beams and doors can often be found in great numbers. Old metal fixtures such as railings, windows, and gates can be adapted to new uses. But "buyer beware" applies here, too: that beautiful seventeenth-century stone carved mantelpiece may turn out to be a new piece of cast concrete.

More trustworthy sources for unique elements such as doors and gates are true antiques dealers, usually located in bigger cities. They're often willing to search out particular items for you. Their pieces come with provenances, and they have a reputation to protect, so you can be pretty sure you're getting the real thing. Their higher prices naturally reflect the higher level of quality.

Dining room shelves once did duty as a cabinet in a pasta store. The large drawers hold their contents behind heart-shaped windows.

TODI

AS AN ARCHITECTURAL HISTORIAN,

I'm all too aware that most houses have more than

one history. Different owners over the years leave

their mark: making changes and additions, pulling

walls down, building others. In Italy, where history is

told in centuries or even millennia rather than years

and decades, the origins of a building are more likely

than not a far cry from the most recent owners' aims.

But sometimes the two coincide in unexpected ways,

with happy results.

An American art collector and his Italian

companion, an artist, had very specific requirements

when they began their search for a house in Umbria.

One—not easy to come by in typical farmhouses—

was lots of wall space to accommodate their art

collection. From the outset they knew that only a *villa padronale* would suit their needs. Unlike run-of-the-mill farmhouses, which were smallish and incorporated living areas for both man and beast, these mini villas built by landowners were larger and more formal affairs, complete with internal staircases. They're considerably rarer, as there were fewer landowners than farmers.

THE LIVING ROOM WAS EXTENDED beyond the fireplace and is now double its original size, left. The resulting area above the extension, on the second floor, was used to create a terrace off the master bedroom. The artist Ugo Rondinone installed his art along one wall of the room, above, incorporating pine planks, pink plastic film, and speakers that play music in his multimedia work. Previous spread: The rear facade faces an enclosed courtyard; the fountain is topped by a twentieth-century bronze. The brick archway, which mirrors one on the front facade, leads to a spacious central hall where the owners display large-scale sculpture.

But the couple had seen a number of them, from one end of Umbria to the other. As anyone who has looked for a house in Italy can tell you, the challenge is finding a great one in a great location. This house met the challenge perfectly. Located at the end of a road used only for farm access, it offered privacy as well as sweeping views of the tranquil Tiber Valley and the distant Peglia Mountains.

The structure didn't start with its current grand proportions. The original nucleus was built in the sixteenth century by priests from the church in the next village (the house is called Casa dei Frati, "House of the Priests"). Eventually the priests left and the landowners moved in. They added a wing for symmetry and created a grand entrance hall with arches at either end, big enough to let a horse and carriage through.

During the last hundred years, the house has had a more humble life. When the landowners moved out, farmers moved in, turning the grand ground-floor rooms into animal stables. During the tobacco boom of the 1950s, a 10-meter- (33-foot-) tall drying tower was added to the north end of the house. By the time the present owners took over, the place had been abandoned for more than thirty years.

One of the current owners' main objectives was to restore and emphasize the formality and symmetry of the original *villa padronale*. They opened up the internal staircase, which had been closed by the farmers to separate the downstairs stalls from the living quarters on the second floor. They also kept the classic symmetry of the ground floor, which centered on the entrance hall and was flanked by three rooms on either side.

The owners further formalized the layout by creating an enclosed courtyard between

TWO PAIRS OF DOUBLE GLASS DOORS, opposite, lead from the living room to a newly created terrace paved in terra-cotta tiles. The wrought-iron furniture by Uno Piu is reserved for cocktails when sunsets take center stage. The dining area, above, opens off a terrace complete with an outdoor table and grill. A brick arch (just visible to the left) leads to the kitchen.

the main house and the sixteenth-century outbuilding that is now an artist's studio. Low brick walls define this cloisterlike garden, which is planted simply with geometrically shaped parterres of clipped grass. A low circular basin acts as a central fountain in this secret garden. Even when the cold winds sweep down from the mountains, the garden is protected and offers a green oasis all year.

The only change in the original floor plan was to combine three rooms in the south wing into a new living room. But the space still felt cramped. Building an addition was forbidden by the local planning commission, as it would have increased the volume of the house. The answer was to "delete" volume from another part of the house so it could be "transferred" to the living room addition. This was accomplished by opening up the top floor of the tobacco drying tower and turning it into a terrace.

Throughout the two-year reconstruction of the house, there were several surprise finds. While dismantling the old bread oven, the owners came across a centuries-old altar, an indication of where the priest's chapel had been. The most exciting discovery was made in the garden, below the courtyard. When masons began to pave a terraced area near the house, they broke through what they at first thought was an underground cavern. But they soon realized they had stumbled upon two enormous underground stone cisterns built by the priests to collect water from a nearby spring. That spring, first found by the priests and then lost for decades, has been lovingly restored. Flowing into a stone basin, the water has brought the owners' land to life once more, creating a lush and manicured landscape that surrounds their own version of a *villa padronale*. ∎

A BEADED CURTAIN by artist Felix Gonzales-Torres serves as the door to the powder room on the ground floor, next to the living room, opposite, above. A drawing by Ford Beckman hangs in the master bath, opposite, below. The owners found the 1940s sconce in a local antiques store. The largest of three guest rooms, above, is on the second floor, next to what used to be the tobacco-drying tower. Three steps lead out to the new covered terrace. Following spread: The prefabricated oval swimming pool has one endless edge, so that the division between water and landscape is seamless. A sand-colored lining allows the water to appear pale blue. Stone paving surrounds the rest of the pool and widens just enough at one end to accommodate four lounge chairs. The lawn, planted with olive trees, gives way to worked fields and woods. Rather than build a shade structure such as a covered pergola, the home owners chose to rely on nature: oak and elm trees provide a cool respite from the bright afternoon sun.

VOLUMI

VOLUME RESTRICTIONS

One of the most attractive aspects of Italian life is the laissez-faire attitude to just about everything. Italians are nothing if not accommodating, and adhering to strict rules is almost unheard of. In fact, most citizens seem to regard laws as suggestions—to be considered, certainly, but with a good dose of interpretation thrown in.

This anything goes attitude has been generously applied to building regulations, sometimes with horrific results. The economic boom in the fifties and sixties saw an explosion of construction. In the south especially, but also in the peripheries of major cities, the motto was "If you can afford it, you can build it." Large-scale construction—apartment buildings, hotels, factories—that had little to do with the surrounding countryside or architecture sprang up, with or without permits, ruining many existing landscapes and cityscapes in the process.

Thankfully, large areas of the countryside, which are too remote to have been attractive for financial development, have remained pristine. Recognizing their responsibility to protect this natural resource, local building commissions have finally begun to enact tougher building codes to limit new construction (see page 68). In some areas the rules are particularly tough, requiring an enormous quantity of land for new development. Elsewhere, even this option is forbidden to all but local farmers, to discourage rampant land speculation and development.

In areas where the laws are strictest—Umbria and Tuscany are two of the more prominent—the only way to "build" a home is to restore a ruin. Even though there may be little more than four walls and a rotting roof, the owner is buying the "footprint" and the right to reconstruct what was once there. The only restrictions are that the restored building have the same volume as the original building and that new additions be limited to about 10 percent of the original volume.

But there are still ways to bend these strict rules. The owners of the *villa padronale* took down the external walls of the top floor of their tobacco drying tower and turned it into an open terrace (right). Karen Wolman and Baruch Ben Chorin had all the medieval ruins on their property—potential building volume—surveyed and entered on the official maps and deeds (see page 190). Although they have no immediate plans to restore them, they or their heirs will have that option in the future.

Another way to increase the volume of an established ruin is to dig down. Over the years, the ground level of old buildings tends to rise as the elements wash mud and dirt nearer to the house. Foundations become submerged, and even the interiors, which are usually dirt floors, rise. Digging several feet down, both inside and out, often makes cramped, inaccessible ground floor rooms spacious and useful once again without flying in the face of building restrictions.

TORRE GENTILE

CONVERTING A RUINED FARMHOUSE

into a home is one thing. Converting a whole ruined

village is off most people's radar. The nucleus of

Villanova, the property Karen Wolman bought, is a

farmhouse built from stones salvaged from a medieval

village that had burnt to the ground in the twelfth

century. Surrounding it were the walls and towers of

the town itself, so covered with brambles and vines that

she wasn't even quite sure what she had purchased.

What she thought she knew for certain was that

the house would need little work as it had been

recently inhabited. The reality was quite the opposite:

the structure had to be practically gutted and rebuilt

from the inside out.

Karen, an American journalist living in Rome at the time, came to visit Domenico and me at a house we had rented just outside of Todi one summer. When she expressed a desire to sink some rustic roots, Domenico said he knew just the house for her. Set in a small hamlet, the little farmhouse had just enough land for a garden and a pool. It was private enough for her needs, but not completely isolated from neighbors.

THE KITCHEN IS SPACIOUS ENOUGH to eat in, left. Cabinetry was custom-made by a carpenter in Rome; the countertops are oak. A large fireplace, above, was made from salvaged stones from northern Umbria. In the sitting room beyond is a mantelpiece imported from England. Previous spread: A wide gravel-topped path, shaded by an ancient elm, leads to the front door, where a Mermaid Rose has already established itself. The original external staircase was eliminated, but the upper landing was retained and converted into a covered terrace. Terra-cotta planters full of bright red geraniums keep things colorful as well as providing a safety barrier for adventuresome children.

A DOORWAY CONNECTING the kitchen and the living room, above, was partly walled up, leaving a "window" between the two rooms. Another newly built fireplace, made from salvaged stones and old wooden beams, is topped by a collection of antique tools. A powder room, through the open door, right, was carved out of space created when the external staircase was removed.

There was, however, one obstacle. Like many Italian farmhouses, this one had more than one current owner. These properties are generally handed down from one generation to the next, which often means that more than one sibling owns pieces of it. Getting warring brothers and sisters to sit down in a notary's office and agree on a selling price can be a daunting task. Karen finally convinced two cousins to sell, and Villanova was hers.

THE WALLS OF MOST of the original animal stalls on the ground floor are of exposed stonework. In the guest room, above, small patches of stone above the bed were left unplastered in order to achieve an almost sculptural affect. Another wall was left totally exposed, opposite, to highlight the superb craftsmanship. Both walls retain the original niches, which were used to store belongings in lieu of more expensive wooden furniture.

Before any renovation plan could be drawn up, the contractor had to find out exactly how many buildings were involved. During the excavation, the submerged village began to take shape. Some walls disintegrated when their vegetal support was ripped away. Others proved to be sturdier, showing their shapes as towers and battlements. Newlywed Karen and her husband, Baruch Ben-Chorin, wanted to restore them all, but their budget

KAREN BOUGHT THE SICILIAN BED at the flea market of Porta Portese in Rome. Made of a chromed pewter alloy, it had to be lengthened to accommodate latter-day sleepers. The master bathroom, above, looks out over the garden through a half-moon window created to fit a salvaged wrought-iron grating. Rather than install wooden cabinet fronts on the masonry sink support, the home owner chose fabric curtains for both aesthetic and economic reasons.

said otherwise. They had to content themselves with registering the buildings' existence with the local planning board so that they or their heirs could restore them in the future if they decided to (see page 188).

In the main house, Domenico suggested sticking to the original floor plan where possible. The biggest changes were the addition of four new bathrooms and an internal staircase between the kitchen and second-floor bedrooms. Creative use was made of the small,

otherwise wasted spaces already there: the guest bathroom and heating room are in an area that was excavated under the original external staircase at the front of the house, and storage space was carved from under the new set of stairs.

Exposed beams and terra-cotta tiles define the ceilings throughout. On the second floor, the beams and tiles were painted to match the walls, in keeping with the original house, in which the upstairs living quarters got more refined and costly treatment than the animal stalls downstairs.

THE SWIMMING POOL, opposite, made of reinforced concrete and painted a pale terra-cotta color, was placed to take full advantage of the ruins of an old tower on the property. The walls now form a secluded seating area, out of the wind. Between the house and the pool, above, is an area covered in gravel. The space under the pergola is paved with stones, providing a solid support for the marble-topped table and wrought-iron chairs.

GIARDINI

One of the greatest joys of restoring a country house comes after the contractors have finally left. That's when it's time to turn your personal construction site into a garden. Even the most urban converts to country life start getting itchy green thumbs when faced with raw earth. From the beginning, Karen Wolman and her husband envisioned their garden as an integral part of their home. They knew that they would be spending the warm summer months there, and that much of family life would take place *al fresco*. They were lucky they had a romantic framework to work with—a disintegrating tower and several ruined walls encouraged thoughts of climbing roses and wisteria—but they needed to add many new decorative and structural elements as well.

The endless sunshine of an Italian summer can sometimes be a case of too much of a good thing, which is why the pergola (see pages 165, 201) is an omnipresent structure in Italian gardens. At its simplest, a pergola is four or more poles stuck in the ground and topped with a superstructure made of lighter wooden poles and sometimes bamboo matting; this supports a leafy canopy of climbing vines to provide shade. Karen used chestnut poles, which are resistant to the elements, and wisteria and trumpet vine, deciduous climbers that lose their leaves in winter, allowing the sun to hit the kitchen walls.

With summers that are long, dry, and hot, most of the flowering bushes and trees reach their colorful prime in the spring. To extend that color through July and August, Karen followed the lead of the farmers next door and arranged pots of annuals under the pergola, as well as by the entryway and poolside area. Red geraniums, petunias, and impatiens, planted in handmade terra-cotta pots from nearby Ripabianca, hum with bees and butterflies.

With water shortages common during the summer, keeping acres of grass emerald green isn't very practical. Karen has kept the grassy areas to a minimum—near the pool and in one corner of the garden overlooking the view of Todi. Nearer the house is a terrace paved with stones found on the property. The courtyard and pathways are gravel laid over a weed-repressing layer of polyurethane.

A small courtyard was most likely once another animal stall. Karen Wolman has taken advantage of its shady position to plant a hydrangea bed and walnut tree.

Karen and Baruch found many of the house's decorative elements in England. A set of teak library doors, bought at auction in London, was installed on the second floor. The bold bathroom and kitchen tiles came from Mexico via a store in northwest London. The color of the walls, all warm shades of ocher and yellow, were created by mixing the pigments directly into the plaster, a technique used throughout the house.

But it's in the garden that the greatest changes have been made. From what was once a tangled and mysterious mess has emerged a romantic oasis set within massive ancient walls. The centerpiece is a stone wall that separates the three distinct areas of the garden: the pool, the eating area, and a lawn. A crumbling tower is filled with roses, and a half-ruined courtyard is a hideaway for a hydrangea bed. So intense was Karen's joy at planning this garden that she took a year-long course at London's Royal Horticultural Society; adapting her British knowledge of plants to the arid Umbrian climate has been a challenge. The biggest treat came when she began clearing trees at the far end of the property. Miraculously, a perfect view of Todi opened up, with the cupola designed by Renaissance architect Donato Bramante in the sixteenth century forming the backdrop to the garden. ■

A HANDMADE terra-cotta urn perches on top of one of the many stone walls in the garden, above right. Bright purple petunias bloom all summer long. Below right: An ancient ivy and a stone wall are so intertwined that if one were to be removed, the other would fall.

ROME

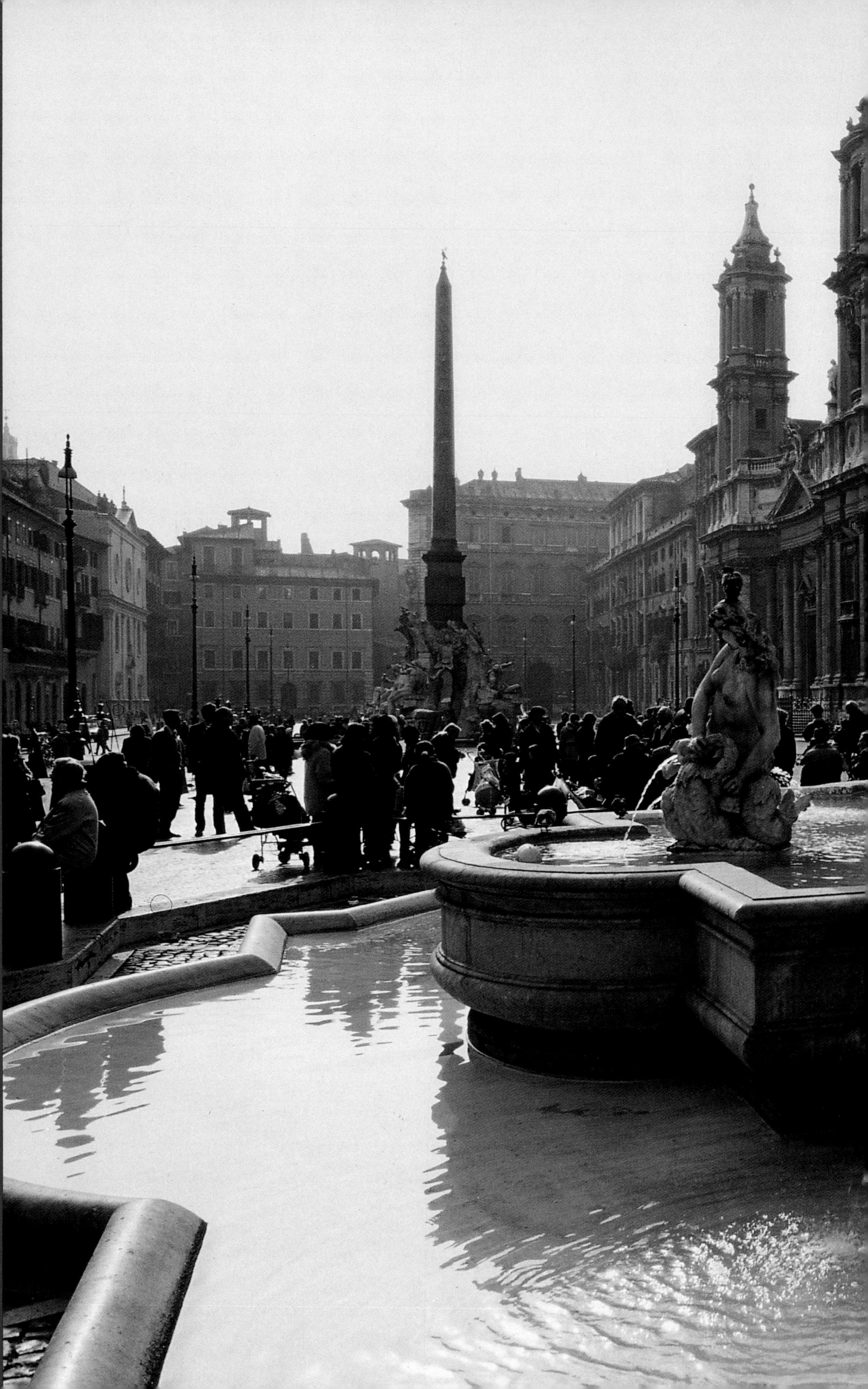

A CANDLE FACTORY IN

TRASTEVERE

ROME IS A CITY OF LAYERS—

of textures, of colors, of past lives. One of the reasons

it has no major subway system is that the minute

spades are laid to earth, another ruin is discovered. I'm

still amazed when I drop my daughter off at grade

school every day—a few yards from the Colosseum.

Much of the charm of Rome is that modern life

goes on amid its treasures. Marble columns and por-

ticoes, baroque domes and portals, become a backdrop

to everyday life. And while it would be easy to take

such beauty for granted, I don't think anyone ever does.

The house in which Giorgio and Gaia Franchetti

now live is in Trastevere, an area of the city separated

from the historic center by the Tiber River. (*Trastevere*

means "across the Tiber.") In ancient times this was

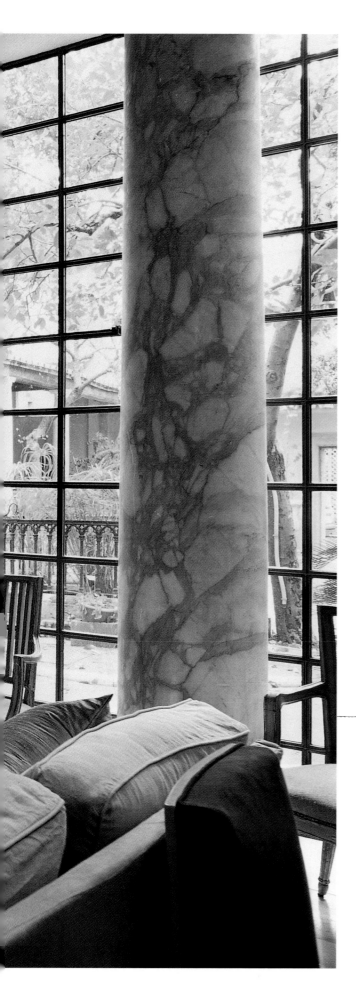

FLOOR-TO-CEILING WINDOWS in the living room, left, are reminders of the building's days as a candle factory. The walls, painted a bright saffron, contrast with the deep red velvet curtains and reflect Gaia's love of the strong Indian palette. The door frames were painted with a trompe l'oeil technique to mimic marble; the doors themselves are re-creations of a seventeenth-century design. Previous spread: Beyond the iron gates, the surprise is an enclosed garden, complete with vegetable patch. Marble columns support a portico, giving the space a Roman feeling. The pathways are made of a variety of materials: small square cobblestones, rectangular slabs of porous *tufo*, and a checkerboard mix of stone and brick.

still countryside, and even up until the seventeenth and eighteenth centuries, Romans built hunting lodges and summer cottages along the green hill of the Janiculum, which rises from the banks of the river. In the nineteenth and twentieth centuries, the area gave way to small-scale industry, and factories began to line the streets along the river. Until recently, the area was still considered "marginal"; a large prison didn't help its

THE FLOOR OF THE HALLWAY off the living room, above left, is made of fragments of ancient Roman marble. A stenciled pattern that repeats an Indian design borders the ceiling of the study, above right. Opposite: In a small sitting room on the ground floor, antique terra-cotta tiles, each one a slightly different hue, cover the floor. The coffered ceiling is painted a bright turqouise blue, and the trompe l'oeil painting on each square reproduces a different type of colored marble. The seventeenth-century fireplace was installed by the home owners.

reputation. (At night, prisoners could be heard calling messages to their wives in the road below!) The building the Franchettis bought, last used as a candle factory, was itself less than inviting, its courtyard cluttered with machinery and large metal vats.

Although parts of the building date from the seventeenth century, most of the structure dates from the 1920s, when the area was still a thriving industrial zone. The three wings of the house wrap around the large courtyard, where fires were built to heat the vats of candle wax, and all of the windows face inward. The only breach in the streetside facade is the large entrance gate.

Rather than open up more windows, which could have taken in views of the Janiculum Hill above, Giorgio chose to preserve the 1920s structure, creating his own version of a patrician house. In ancient Rome, private homes were built around an *impluvium*, or courtyard, which was open to the elements so that rainwater could collect in its center fountain. This house contains not only a fountain but a symmetrically laid out garden as well. To further emphasize the Roman feeling, Giorgio transformed a utility shed into a portico with

IN GAIA'S DESIGN STUDIO on the second floor, opposite, immense windows overlook the inner courtyard and flood the room with light. Brightly colored cottons and silks are piled high on the table and stacked in cupboards. The master bedroom, above, opens on to a small rooftop terrace. The rooms are especially large and spacious, with high ceilings throughout—a rarity in this ancient Roman neighborhood.

the addition of massive marble columns, which his father had found in the 1930s.

In the course of construction, the Franchettis had a happy surprise. During routine digging to install a modern plumbing system, workers unearthed a Roman floor mosaic. It was most likely the centerpiece of a patrician house dating from the first century B.C.

The Roman fragments were romantic finds, but the building's industrial side had its strengths as well. The Franchettis took full advantage of the high ceilings to create large and spacious rooms, rare in this city. Equally attractive were the large expanses of wall space—the windows were limited to one side of the house—which gave Giorgio, who is one of Italy's best-known collectors of contemporary art, ample space to display his treasures. Several of the existing windows are large framed industrial ones overlooking the courtyard; many go from floor to ceiling, the strong Roman sunlight blocked by heavy curtains.

If the house's structure and sense of Roman classicism are mostly due to Giorgio, it is Gaia who is responsible for the home's vivid color scheme. Strong tones are everywhere, from the walls to the ceilings and even the cement on the floors. After years of making documentary films in India, Gaia found she was increasingly drawn to the textiles and art of the country, and during restoration of the house, she realized that in many ways Giorgio's sense of Roman classicism was not so different from much of her own Indian aesthetic. She eventually began to develop a line of home fabrics that combined the two, using her own home as the testing ground. In her office on the second floor, overlooking the courtyard, she designs fabrics rich in strong Pompeiian reds and saffron yellows that will be hand-loomed in India. ■

THE FACADES OF THE BUILDINGS in Trastevere don't tell the whole story of what lies within. A surprising element of the Franchetti house is the inner courtyard, a charming bit of urban green. A small fountain, surrounded by papyrus plants, acts as the centerpiece. The paving is a handmade brick and larger slabs of stone.

SPAZI INDUSTRIALI

The view from the portico of the Franchetti courtyard takes in the facade of the living room and a study on the right. The one-story wing houses the dining room and kitchen.

The idea of turning an industrial space into living quarters was not a common one in Italy until very recently. Although adventurous artists in Rome and Milan had begun to reclaim old pasta factories as studio space, the trend was not nearly so established as it was in the United States or Britain. Today, an increasing number of Italians are taking this route, although the phenomenon seems mostly restricted to urban areas. In the countryside, many of these buildings—magnificent turn-of-the-century brick structures, "newer" buildings dating from the 1920s and 1930s, former pasta factories, mills—remain abandoned, as these kinds of structures aren't often on the local real estate agent's list of homes. One reason may be their less than tranquil locations. Convenience dictated that factories be as near as possible to transportation routes, which may mean that railroad tracks or a road runs past the front door. Other buildings, such as mills, may border the banks of out-of-the-way rivers or streams. Prospective buyers have to be more inventive to track down these properties.

John Martin, a British architect who specializes in industrial restorations in England and has recently begun scouting projects in Italy, believes this kind of conversion hasn't caught on in Italy because both the populace and the financial institutions are conservative, and it takes a while for a trend like this to take hold. Still, these buildings are bound to be snapped up sooner or later. With traditional farmhouses becoming ever more difficult to find, industrial spaces are sure to become the next hot item in Italian housing.

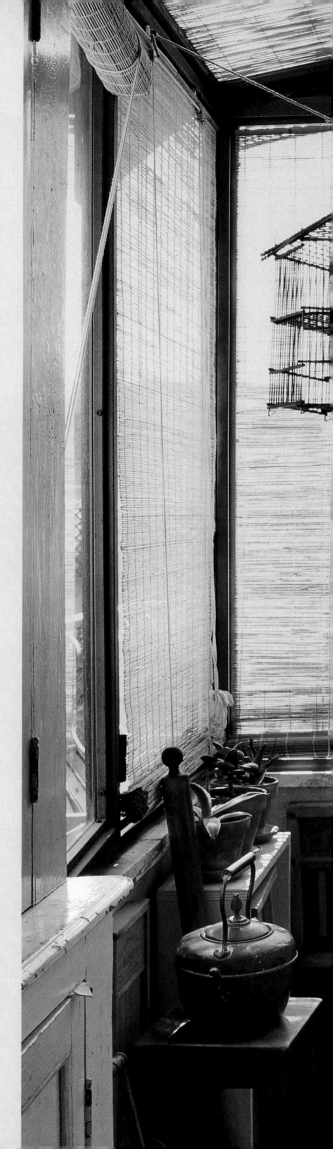

A ROOFTOP APARTMENT ON

VIA MONSERRATO

ONE OF THE ALL-TIME GREAT

tricks of the trade of Italian interior design is decorative

painting. From Etruscan tombs to Michelangelo's

Sistine ceiling and right on up to the faux marble

work on modern-day tables and chairs, Italians have

specialized in making surfaces almost disappear

beneath a layer of skillfully applied paint. In fact, it

was the seductive and illusionist effects of Renaissance

decorative painting that were partly responsible for

my ending up living in Italy. I had gone to Florence to

study and research the Medici gardens. Although dec-

orative painting doesn't immediately spring to mind

in the context of gardens, it was the use of such paint-

ing there that led me to explore the sixteenth-century

grottoes in the Boboli Gardens. I found man-made caves where the walls seemed to melt away beneath a breathtaking mix of painting, stucco work, and sculpture created by some of the leading artists of the day.

Ursula Franco, a young decorator in Rome, decided to use decorative crafts to make her Roman attic apartment appear to be more than it is. After six years of practicing medicine, she abandoned the field and followed her childhood dreams. She enrolled in Rome's famed school of decorative arts, the Accademia Del Superfluo, and worked for several years as director Roberto Lucifero's assistant. She seriously considered becoming an interior designer for a time but chose instead to focus on decorative painting. She liked the idea that with relatively little money, spaces could be magically transformed.

Her apartment has become a sort of template of all that the decorative field has to offer. When she bought the 70-square-meter (750-square-foot) attic, the space was like a time capsule from the seventies. Although the building itself dates from the fifteenth century, the most recent owner had played free and loose with wall-to-wall carpeting, mirrors, and drab colors. Additions made to the building over the centuries spread the apartment out over five levels. The first step was to remove all the internal doors to open up the space, create a flow, and make the rooms appear bigger than they are.

Ursula's next project was to prepare the walls for decoration. Rather than carefully smoothing out all cracks and bumps, she left them uneven and almost lumpy, as they might have looked centuries before. Then she applied her designs in *finto affresco*, or fake fresco, a technique that uses water-

AN OLD OAK TABLE in one corner of the kitchen, topped with a slab of white Carrara marble, creates a breakfast nook, above. The home owner, a self-professed hoarder of objects, can see decorating a house in minimalist style—for someone else. The small terrace, opposite, is just big enough for a table for two and some heat-loving plants; the dome of Saint Peter's is visible on the horizon. Previous spread: The minuscule kitchen used to be a rooftop terrace. Slatted bamboo blinds help keep the hot Roman sun at bay. Innumerable garage sale finds are displayed against a delicate mauve background.

AFFRESCHI

When the great masters of the Renaissance painted their works on the walls of churches, villas, and palaces, they used a technique called *affresco*—"fresh" in Italian, which refers to the plaster on which they painted. Drawings called cartoons were meticulously prepared to scale for the entire surface. Each day a section of plaster would be applied to the wall, and while the fresco was still wet, or "fresh," the cartoon for that section would be transferred to the surface and its outlines filled in with pure pigments. Since the pigments would adhere only to the wet plaster, which dried within twenty-four hours, no more than small sections, called *giornate* ("days") were painted at one time. And since the pigments themselves changed as they dried, complete mastery of the palette was essential: the artist had to understand the chemistry of each color and what its final effect would be.

True fresco is a very difficult method that doesn't allow for any mistakes or changes. The technique that Ursula Franco chose, called *finto affresco*, or fake fresco, is similar but more forgiving. Like true fresco, it uses pure pigments, but they're mixed with *grassello di calce*, or lime, to give body and texture to the colors. And like real fresco, the pigments reveal their true colors only when completely dry. But with *finto affresco* the artist can paint freehand on already prepared dry walls and not be bound by the time constraints of the day's fresh plaster patch.

Nina Eaton, a decorative painter who works in both Italy and the United States, describes another form of *finto affresco* that allows even more freedom. In this case, a wall is prepared and the plaster left to dry, then sanded down to give it a rough surface. Painting is done with either acrylics or simple wall paint. Further "distressing" to give an aged look can be carried out at the end of the process by roughing up the surface with sandpaper. There are also many new products, such as glazes, that can add a transparent coat of color to further "age" the painting.

The bright shade of yellow in Ursula Franco's dining room looks completely modern, but is in fact a shade that was popular in the fifteenth century.

based acrylic paints in a thick layer that conveys even more texture to the surface.

For the kitchen, Ursula chose an eighteenth-century shade of mauve, dappled and applied with a light touch, to form the background. The dining room, which is actually on a sort of loft overlooking the entrance/studio, presented unique difficulties. She had originally wanted to paint faux curtains that "wrapped" themselves around the space, but the sloping roofline made it impossible to fit in this design. Instead, she used a damask pattern dating from the fifteenth century, which she copied from a sixteenth-century altarpiece. The vivid yellows were chosen to brighten up the rather dark room.

The bedroom is Ursula's reinterpretation of an eighteenth-century oriental room. Although small, the space is well proportioned, which allowed her to create a complex design. Since she couldn't quite decide between a Chinese and a Japanese theme, she devised a classic Chinese framework across which Japanese geishas dance.

The work done in the bathroom is a perfect example of the ease and economy of decorative painting. The pattern mimics the Arab tiles from the Alhambra in Spain. Real majolica tiles would have been prohibitively expensive, as well as hard to install; the painted version is inexpensive and cheerful

A R E N A I S S A N C E pattern was reproduced on the dining room walls, right. The room is illuminated only by candlelight; by night the work desk is transformed into a romantic and shadowy dining table. The loftlike space that overlooks the painting studio, above right, is reached by a flight of steep wooden stairs. It also doubles as the entrance to the apartment.

THE BEDROOM, above, is the only square room in the apartment, and the only one with an even ceiling, making it the easiest to decorate. Using a neutral backdrop with such clean proportions allowed for a complicated design of elaborately costumed geishas posing against a border of rectilinear Chinese patterns. The mirrored door visually expands the small room. The bathroom, opposite, is an exotic exploration of Arab tile patterns: everything has been painted except for the marble tiles around the tub. The tasseled linen curtain, designed and made by the home owner, repeats the colors of the tiles.

and can always be changed should she grow tired of the design.

But in the long run, what convinced Ursula to buy the apartment was the room to which she has added none of her own touches: the terrace. It's small, but it's where she spends the better part of her day, even in the winter.

"I love what I do," Ursula says. "And I adore the interiors I've created. But who can compete with this?" she adds, pointing to the dome of Saint Peter's in the distance, glowing pink against the setting Roman sun. ∎

VIA DEL CORSO

ONE OF THE REASONS I LOVE living in Rome is that nothing ever really changes. Despite a superficial layer of urban chaos, the sense of history and continuity is all-enveloping and reassuring. Not only are these the same unchanged streets that I walked as a child some thirty years ago; on some you can still trace the tracks of Roman chariots.

Yet for all its static facades and monuments, there's a side of Rome that's forever changing. Maybe because the architectural framework itself is so permanent, people are constantly coming up with new ways to use these ancient buildings. The previous owners of our apartment in Rome had chickens roosting in what is now our bedroom. Our favorite

restaurant is located in what was once a Roman amphitheater, complete with massive stone columns. Palaces once belonging to Roman nobility have long since been divided into shops and apartments. Looking at real estate in this city requires a mind open to the possibilities, not the restrictions.

For Andrea Truglio, a Rome-based interior designer, the first glimpse of what would become his home wasn't about possibilities. It was about pure repulsion! When he first saw the apartment, located on central Rome's main artery, the via del Corso, it was being used as a *sartoria*, a tailor's workshop. It was big by Rome standards—more than 150 square meters (1,600 square feet)—but the space was divided up into a seemingly endless warren of tiny cubicles: sewing rooms, pressing rooms, and dressing rooms for the clients. Andrea discovered that the multitudes of corridors and walls were only temporary and that in fact only four structural pilasters supported the 3.4-meter-high (11-foot) ceilings. Envisioning wide-open spaces reminiscent of New York lofts, he took a leap of faith and moved in.

TWO WINDOWS look out on the busy via del Corso, but serenity reigns in the living room, right, where the colors are all pastel hues. The wide teak floor planks were cut irregularly and installed with nails rather than the more modern method of using glue. The fireplace is purely for show; it's made of wood, covered in plaster, and painted to resemble stone. Previous spread: A floor-to-ceiling mirror creates the illusion of space and extends the living room beyond its walled boundaries. All of the plaster architectural details, including columns, friezes, and baseboards, were designed by the home owner.

First to go, of course, were all the partitions, which were not only fracturing the space but blocking the sunlight from the floor-to-ceiling windows overlooking the street. The next step was to figure out how to keep this feeling of openness and light while carving out living and working quarters. The four supporting pilasters were there to stay, so Andrea worked around them. He kept the more public spaces—living room and study—at the front of the apartment, near

OPEN SHELVING SEPARATES THE LIVING ROOM, left, from the entrance hall. An ever-changing collection of vases and architectural models filters the light that comes through the pair of windows at the other end of the living room. The table in the entrance hall, above, doubles as a dining table. The curtains on the left hide a small storage area, and the curtains on the right lead to the front door.

the light. The more private areas—bedroom and bathroom—are located in the back, in the partial shadows created by the new partitions. A new entryway doubles as a dining room and work area, where Andrea alternately hosts dinner parties and meets with clients. It was tempting to keep the entire space open, but he chose to separate this "room" from the more formal salon with open shelving. In this way he got a separate entrance while allowing the light from the front windows to shine through.

At first glance, the sleek cool interiors seem far removed from the world of grand piazzas and palaces outside. Not so, claims Andrea. Most people think of the city as a patchwork of terra-cottas and ochers, when in fact up until quite recently the buildings were beautifully tinted with pastel colors. The gray-blue walls of Andrea's living room are the exact shade used for many building exteriors in eighteenth-century Rome; unlike darker earth tones, which absorb light, this color reflects the changing tones of the Roman day. Sometimes cool, often warm, the walls bring a bit of the changing seasons and the times of the day into the apartment.

THE STUDY, opposite, opens off the living room. A built-in desk is wide enough to double as a drafting table; the bookshelves hold a collection of reference books on design. "Since this space is both my home and my office," says the home owner, "there is a curious mix of both reticence and experimentation." Sober forms define the furnishings he designed, while the violet velvet on the sofa, above left, adds a touch of humor to the room. Slatted shuttered doors, below left, lead to the bedroom.

ARTIGIANI

The kitchen in the via del Corso apartment is made to seem bigger by rather grand furnishings. An eighteenth-century Austrian portrait dominates, and a banquette and two chairs designed by the home owner provide seating for four.

Although the twenty-first century has definitely arrived in Rome, the city still boasts the small workshops that have lined its alleyways since ancient times. While rising rents, especially in the historic center, are slowly pushing these small-scale businesses to the outskirts, for the time being at least, many are still holding on. From my apartment I can hear blasts of a trumpet from the wind-instrument repairman, the grinding wheel of the knife sharpener, the slow and steady beat of the cobbler's hammer—the sounds that make every neighborhood in Rome a village unto itself.

One of the great tools of interior designer Andrea Truglio's trade is his access to the artisans of Rome. It is only very recently, for example, that ready-made furniture stores have made inroads in Italy. Furniture was, and in most cases still is, something ordered from a carpenter, an upholsterer, or even a metalsmith. Andrea depends on these artisans, whom he refers to as his "team," to make his visions a reality.

Some of the most important members of that team are the painters, because color plays such a fundamental role in every Italian restoration. Living in Italy isn't like living in Paris or New York, where electric light is predominant and effects can be controlled. Here it's almost impossible to pick a color from a paint sample. Instead you must apply paint to the walls and watch it as the light passes across it over the course of a day.

The Negri brothers, painters who have long collaborated with Andrea, have decades of experience on projects from grand palaces to small apartments to country houses and seaside villas. When the designer has a vision of, say, the fleeting color of a Roman sunset, it is the Negri brothers who are able to capture the moment and fix it forever in paint.

Andrea has also harnessed the skill of craftsmen who practice the ancient art of stuccowork. Whether it is a severe geometric frieze or a simple pilaster, he has used the three-dimensional effects of this art to add depth and texture to his interiors.

Taking full advantage of skilled Roman artisans, Andrea had stucco friezes, columns, and cornices created to frame windows, doors, and walls. The details are classic Greek in inspiration. Abstract sun-shaped disks form a minimalist dado around the cornice of the living room; the pilasters, which flank the doorways leading from the entryway and connecting the living room and study, are pared-down Doric. An archway separates the living room and study, a room with two large windows. A built-in desk and bookshelves define the office space, where linen panels cover four bookshelves.

The bathtub is set on a black marble plinth directly in the middle of a wall in the bedroom. Instead of completely closing off the room, Andrea chose Caribbean-inspired slat-worked doors to let in light all day.

It is the ever-changing light reflected off the carefully colored walls that is the most important element in Andrea's home. "While construction is what holds things up and binds things together, and the floor plan is what effects the flow, it is actually the surface decoration that is applied last and almost superficially that makes all the difference," says the designer. "Color is very important. Besides being able to hide any flaws that couldn't be solved architecturally, it also gives body to the illusion." ∎

THE HOME OWNER designed most of the apartment's pared-down furnishings, including a minimal bed, above right. The bathtub, located in the master bedroom, below right, is set on a black marble base. Two built-in closets stand on either side. A smaller bath with toilet and sink is located down the hall.

SOUTH

MATERA

MATERA, A SMALL TOWN IN Basilicata in southern Italy, is unlike any other city I've ever visited. Inhabited since the seventh century, the historic center of the town, called I Sassi, is built up along two large stone ravines and is based on a complex system of cave dwellings that were dug out from a soft chalky stone called *tufo*. As the caves were enlarged by digging out more rooms from the living rock, the resulting excavated blocks of stone were used to construct new rooms that projected out from the hillside.

These unique dwellings flourished and prospered until the 1930s, when efforts by bureaucrats to "modernize" the neighborhoods resulted in paving over the open waterways that had collected and harnessed rainwater for centuries. The new system of

grottoes and cisterns was deemed unhygienic; unfortunately, not much else was done to bring plumbing up to standards, and squalor soon reigned. Poverty increased to such an extent that people were sharing caves with farm animals, and the delicate ecosystem that had prospered for more than a thousand years fell into severe decay. The situation was considered a national disgrace. In the 1950s I Sassi were deemed beyond redemption, and a law was passed ordering the inhabitants to move into newly built modern apartments at the town's periphery.

Like most Italians, I had a preconception of Matera based on slightly sinister memories. My father visited there in the 1970s,

T H E   H E A V Y   F R O N T   D O O R ,   opposite, was made by a local carpenter and is set into the ancient facade, which is carved of large slabs of *tufo* excavated from the inner caves of the house. The courtyard, open to the elements, serves as the entry hall. Above left: The fireplace, a new addition to one of the oldest parts of the house, is sculpted from a local stone called *mazzaro* using a technique that doesn't require cement. Above right: The rooms are cavelike, and on many different levels, connected by stairs cut into the living stone. Previous spread: A balcony on the second floor overlooks the house's inner courtyard on one side and the town on the other.

when it was basically a ghost town. But he found something magical about the empty caves and echoing streets. The strong impression the town made on him transferred itself to me, and for years I tried to find an excuse to go there. By the time I did, things had changed quite a bit. After suffering decades of neglect and abandon by local inhabitants, I Sassi had been brought back to life partly thanks to international attention.

An architect and native son, Pietro Laureano, was instrumental in focusing global interest in their preservation. In 1992, he and his wife, Astier, returned to Matera, where they rented a small apartment in I Sassi. During the course of the year, while he wrote his proposal for UNESCO to place Matera on the World Heritage List, the couple fell sway to the neighborhood's charms. The lack of cars provided a traffic- and pollution-free environment, and the beauty and the architecture of the place convinced them to call it home. Eventually, they decided to find a building to restore themselves. Although many of the buildings, grottoes, and caves appear at first glance to be abandoned, many still belong to someone, and it's not easy tracking down the owners. During the fifties, when most of the inhabitants were encouraged to move out, the municipality took possession of many of the abandoned dwellings, which entered into the public domain. Others, often owned by several members of the same family, remained in private hands. Still others were taken over by squatters who claimed ownership rights.

After untangling the bureaucratic web of ownership, Pietro bought the main part of his house from a private seller. Tacked onto the original above-ground structure is an extensive network of caves, cisterns, and

THE LIVING ROOM, opposite, is in the most ancient part of the house, cut into the stone of the hillside. Beneath the floor are large cisterns that were used to hold water. Above: The rear wall of the living room boasts niches that probably held offerings as part of an ancient shrine. The canal cut into the wall, perhaps Neolithic, was used to drain and collect rainwater. The walls are covered in a special type of plaster that decreases the buildup of humidity, a technique that dates back to the first century A.D.

THE MASTER BEDROOM, above, is on the "newer" second floor—dating to the seventeenth century. Antique bricks had been laid in a herringbone pattern on the floor but were hidden under a layer of cement and terra-cotta tiles. Blocks of local *tufo* were used on the vaulted ceiling. Opposite: A Turkish bath was created within one of the cisterns. The sunken tub is lined with tiles from Vietri, near Naples. Many other cisterns and rooms in the house still await restoration—"a continuing process requiring time, patience, and the vision and energy to see it through," say the home owners.

grottoes, all part of the public domain, which the Laureanos have leased from the state for ninety-nine years.

The couple began restoring the cavernous space to the natural refuge it originally was. One of the main problems was that over the years the immense cisterns under the house, which were originally used to hold water, had been filled in with rubble. The result was that the ground floors had become dank and humid. Once they were painstakingly cleared out, the house was allowed to breathe once more.

ACQUA

An ancient niche carved into a side wall of the Laureano grotto forms a well at the base, where capillary action enabled the original inhabitants to collect water. At a certain time every day, sunlight streaks through the front door and hits this spot directly in the center.

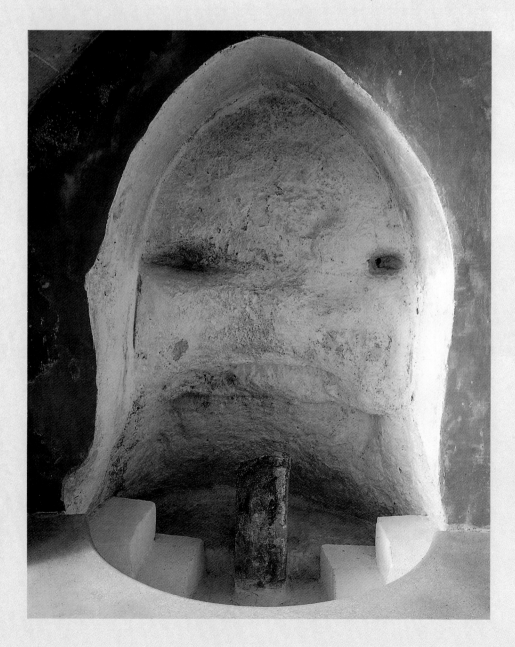

Urban restorations don't present water management problems, since apartments are connected to city water systems. But venture out into the countryside and the situation is much different.

In the past, isolated farmhouses usually depended upon a local source for water. A spring or a well often provided what small needs the family had. The home own-ers on page 178 discovered ancient cisterns that fed their own spring still running strong after at least four hundred years.

Not everyone is so lucky. When we moved into our house in Umbria, we had no water source at all. During the first year, a truck made weekly visits to fill up two 10,000-liter (2,700-gallon) underground cisterns with water that we'd pump up to the house. After a year of paying really high water bills, we decided to try to dig a well. That's when we discovered there was no scientific method for deciding where to start. Instead, this impor-tant information was provided by a group of three diviners: one with a forked stick, another with a gold ring on the end of a rope, and a mystic in nearby Terni who dreamed we would find water "by a large tree." After two attempts and 180 meters (590 feet), we gave up. We have now connected to the local aqueduct, which fills our cisterns.

Whether you're getting your water from a well or from the local water company, it's always good insurance to install at least one large cistern. In most parts of central and southern Italy, water is in short supply during the summer months. Wells tend to go dry, and water companies often impose midday rationing. A holding tank or two will ensure water security for one or more days, depend-ing on the size. So will leading all the drainpipes and gutters from the roof to top off the tank when it rains.

Like most houses in Matera, this one traces an architectural timeline. The main living room, located in the oldest part of the house, is carved right into the rock. Niches in the rear wall date back more than seven hundred years and may have been part of an ancient shrine. The newer parts of the house—the kitchen and upper stories—were built out and up around the original caves in the seventeenth century.

Walking into the house is a surprising experience. It's not cool, dark, or damp but warm and bright and welcoming. The blinding white stone used to front the facade is sculpted in intricate patterns. The bedrooms, with their soaring arched ceilings, are filled with light. The floor in the master bedroom is centuries-old bricks laid down in a complicated herringbone pattern. A central courtyard allows light to pour into the kitchen and living room. The thick walls and natural insulation make the temperature even all year; heating is rarely needed in the winter, and during the summer it's always fresh and cool.

The timeline continues. While as recently as ten years ago you couldn't give away homes in I Sassi, they have now become so sought after that the rising prices have almost put them out of reach. Perhaps it's a blessing that the neighborhood was abandoned and ignored, for while other historic centers have seen the inroads of modernization applied haphazardly over the last forty years, I Sassi appear to have been preserved in a sort of time capsule. Now, when the homes are finally appreciated, people like the Laureanos are helping to bring life to this magical town once more. ■

THE HOME OWNERS CHOSE UNIQUE ELEMENTS for their kitchen, including a deep sink salvaged from an abandoned farm. Rainwater collected in the cisterns, as well as water from the town, runs from the double faucets.

A GROUP OF TRULLI IN

CISTERNINO

PUGLIA, THE REGION LOCATED in the heel of Italy's boot, is far removed from the rest of the country. Despite the intense beauty of the wild landscapes, it's a rare and adventurous foreigner who includes it on his itinerary. For that matter, most Italians know precious little about the area. One of the most fascinating, and perhaps strangest, sights throughout the region are the unique structures known as *trulli*. Exotic and mystical, they appear to have dropped down from outer space.

At its simplest, a *trullo* is made up of a single square room topped by a cone-shaped stone roof, which usually created a loft under the dome. *Trulli* were used to house either animals or people. As families and farms grew, more *trulli* could be constructed adjacent

to the original core, thus forming small groups with interconnecting doors. But each would retain its own cone-shaped roof, so that clusters of them appear to be so many peaked party hats.

Like many farmhouses throughout the country, most *trulli* were abandoned during the decades following World War II. Farmers, the original tenants, chose either to move to more modern, comfortable homes or abandon the land altogether. The *trulli* were either vacated or transformed into animal and tool sheds.

The feelings these small buildings provoke are understandably strong. "It was love at first sight," says Stefania Allegri and her husband, Alessandro, who were simply unsuspecting tourists from Sicily when they spotted their first one. They satisfied their curiosity about these odd buildings by visiting Puglia every summer. Eventually, though, they felt the need to sink their roots deeper. And so began their lifelong affair with bringing these buildings back to life. Over the last fifteen years they have acquired two separate groups of abandoned *trulli* near the town of Cisternino. They transformed one group of four domed buildings into their own private home; the other serves as a small *agriturismo* called Il Portico, a country bed-and-breakfast with six guest rooms. Like most *trulli,* both clusters of buildings had been slowly added to over the centuries. Il Portico is actually made up of eight separate buildings and three *lamie* (barrel-vaulted structures also common in the area), the oldest of which probably dates back to the sixteenth century.

Transforming *trulli* into a vacation home takes a certain amount of imagination and courage. While the buildings are striking and almost sculptural from the exterior, their appearance doesn't translate into easy living

THE LIVING ROOM, above, occupies one of the four *trulli* that make up Stefania and Alessandro's home. The entry hall, separated by a stone archway, is another *trullo;* the wooden loft that now takes up the upper half of the dome is accessible by ladder. The lower archway in the background leads to a niche that became the kitchen. Opposite, above: The entryway to this *trullo,* part of Il Portico and used as a guest suite, has a typical covered porch flanked by two benches. Opposite, below: The tiny kitchen is big enough only for a small table for two. A corner cupboard provides what little storage space there is. Previous spread: The group of *trulli* that now forms Il Portico were originally rural structures, set in the middle of olive groves and pastures. The home owners have added their own civilizing touch: a stone-paved central courtyard featuring a carved fountain constructed from pieces of a baroque building.

in the interior. One of the greatest challenges is the proportions of the rooms, which of course can't be changed. Each one-room structure must remain as it was; no extra rooms or windows may be added, no doorways enlarged. Yet even in the humblest of these dwellings, the low doorways are treated with almost monumental stonework of carefully carved lintels, niches, and archways.

Stefania and Alessandro's renovations were governed by a strict set of rules laid down by the Italian Ministry of Fine Arts, which regulates and limits any proposed changes to the original buildings. (The *trulli* are also on the World Heritage List of protected sites.) The couple was already intent on retaining and restoring all the original elements, and they wanted all the work to be done by hand, as it would have been in the past. Local masons were able to master the intricate stonework, and the home owners did much of the detailed restoration work, such as stripping the wooden lofts and waxing the floors, themselves. All of the outdoor terra-cotta drainage pipes were carefully restored as well.

Much of the original stonework had survived, including massive paving stones from the nearby quarry of Carparo, active since Roman times. The stones, called *chianche,*

LOW ARCHWAYS, opposite, belie the spaciousness inside. The central room includes a dining table as well as a kitchen in the corner. The bedroom is beyond the double doors. Above and below: In the *lamia*—a long and narrow barrel-vaulted structure with a door at one end and a window at the other—the plaster has been stripped away to reveal the exquisite stonework of the soaring ceiling.

were also used in the new pergola-covered walkway and piazza.

Stefania and Alessandro were innovative when it came to adding new elements. One day in the nearby town of Martina Franca, they happened upon what seemed a pile of rubble but turned out to be pieces of a carved entablature from a seventeenth-century palace. They transformed the fragments, carved out of local cream-colored stone, *pietra di trani,* into the octagonally shaped fountain that is the centerpiece of their paved courtyard.

Imagination ruled when it came to the decor of the interiors. The majolica tiles that line the bathrooms were specially ordered from a tile maker in Sicily, the patterns based on a seventeenth-century design. "You can be rigorously authentic only up to a certain point," Stefania explains. "The original *trulli* didn't even have indoor plumbing, much less tiled bathrooms!" ∎

THE CONICAL ROOFS of some of the *trulli* are ringed by narrow terraces, which are perfect for sunbathing, opposite. The tips are whitewashed and capped with fanciful finials. The roofs visible to the lower left are the tops of two of the barrel-vaulted *lamie.* Above left: Restoration was done with traditional materials, including terra-cotta rain gutters and drainpipes. Below left: The entrance to Il Portico is just that: a portico. Columns constructed of local white stone support wrought-iron arches that drip with jasmine, climbing roses, and wisteria. The shady path leads to the central piazza and its bubbling fountain.

TRULLI

Trulli have dotted the Pugliese landscape as far back as anyone can remember. Their origins, however, remain shrouded in mystery. Because they're similar to buildings found near Aleppo, in Turkey, some think they were first built by an immigrant ethnic group from Asia Minor. Others think they may have originated in a primitive Mediterranean culture. The most prevalent opinion is that they were designed by an indigenous people accustomed to working with the stone so abundant in the region. Though it might seem to make more sense for the *trulli* builders to have used wood to create lighter beams and lintel roof structures (as in northern Italian homes), in Puglia large pieces of wood (from pine or chestnut trees) were unavailable. Instead, the builders depended on concentric rings of stones, built up with each new row slightly smaller and resting on the one below, until the final ring formed a point on top. The resulting inward and downward pressure served to keep the roof in place.

Trulli are usually rectangular. The walls are a double thickness of stone, often up to 1.5 meters (5 feet) thick. The inner and outer layers are filled with rubble; no mortar is used. The roof, built into a cupola with narrowing layers of local gray stone, comes to a point and is finished off with a decorative finial, often topped with a ball. They're often decorated with mystical or Christian abstract symbols applied with whitewash. A gutter to collect rainwater runs around the rim; the water, a precious commodity in this arid land, is held in cisterns below the house, accessible from the rooms through an opening in the floor and a bucket on a rope.

There is usually a simple porch at the entrance, sometimes shaded by a stone awning. The interiors often have only one window; niches or alcoves carved into the thick walls are used for sleeping or cooking. In many cases a loft, built of wood, is added at the level where the wall ends and the roof begins. This space, accessible via a ladder, is used for storage or even sleeping.

While single-room examples can still be found, most *trulli* have been added to over the centuries, resulting in clusters of interconnecting *trulli* that form one home.

Trulli are deceptively simple structures whose integrity depends on expert stone masonry. The cross-section shows the thick walls that support the domed roof of the one-room building. A cistern, used to collect rainwater, is located below ground.

OSTUNI

I VISIT PUGLIA TWO TIMES a year, since my husband's family is from the region's capital, Bari. Like all good Italian families, we get together at prescribed holiday times. One visit usually takes place over Christmas. While the weather is even more temperate than in balmy Rome, winter is definitely felt in the brisk winds that sweep in off the sea. Our other visit takes place in the scorching heat of summer, when we spend long days lounging on pristine white beaches on the east coast of the toe of Italy's boot.

So I've seen Puglia during its two most extreme seasons, and I must admit that I had never seen the charms of having a vacation home in this harsh land-scape. But all that changed one spring several years

ago, when I spent six days crisscrossing the region in mid-May. Nothing had prepared me for the pure greenness of the hills and fields. There wasn't a square inch of road-side that wasn't bursting with multicolored wildflowers. The air was perfumed by grasses, lemon blossoms, and thyme. The twisted centuries-old olive trees were planted in deep red earth. Blindingly white buildings were set against an unbelievably blue sky. I finally got it.

Once I'd discovered the seductive side of Puglia, I knew I had to include a typical *masseria* in this book. *Masserie,* found throughout the region, are whitewashed square structures, usually surrounded by several outbuildings and forming the center of estates and working farms. Like the *ville padronali* farther north, these large buildings were most often occupied by landowners. But unlike the villas, their ground floor was usually used as either stables or storage.

The home that Leonardo Mondadori created in Puglia manages to reflect both the

THE BLINDINGLY WHITE, austere facade, above left, was stripped of additions made in the 1950s. The rooftop terrace, below left, overlooks a walled vegetable garden planted with raised beds. Carved stone finials stand at each of the four corners of the roof. "To leave the stone exposed would have looked too rustic," says the architect of the ground-floor living room arches, opposite. "Instead, the plaster was applied in such a way as to reveal the uneven texture of the stone beneath." The floors are made of hand-cut *chianche.* The heating runs beneath the floor. Previous spread: The walled courtyard provides a sheltered climate for citrus trees, which produce fruit almost all year.

harshness and the softness of this land of extremes. To restore his *masseria,* he turned to interior designer Verde Visconti, with whom he had worked on many projects in other parts of the country. The structure itself was in sound shape, but a number of additions made over the years had to be stripped away to reveal the building's original shape. Leonardo wanted to keep a large terrace and balcony added in the 1950s, as they afforded a magnificent view toward the sea. Verde convinced him that they disrupted the monumentality of the facade.

Another exterior feature that needed attention was the courtyard. This vast "piazza,"

A HIGH WINDOW, original to the kitchen, floods the space with sunlight, above. The backsplash design in mustard and black majolica tile is eighteenth century, but the tiles are modern, made in nearby Grottaglie by Franco Fassano. Opposite: The arched doorways of the living room, formerly the stables, were closed in by metal-framed doorways. Small panes of glass give the room the feeling of an orangery.

enclosed by ten-foot-high walls, had been subdivided over the years. Walls were knocked down to open up the space, which now forms the heart of the house. Part of it was then paved with antique *chianche* pavers. Rather than lay them into a cement foundation, which is customary, Verde spaced the stones in such a way that grass grows up in between

THIS GUEST ROOM, above, is in a separate suite on the ground floor, off the courtyard. The canopy bed was designed by the architect. The master bath, right, a study in spacious luxury, is reached by a narrow staircase leading from the master bedroom above. "There are two luxuries in life," says the home owner, "religion and bathrooms."

the cracks, creating a warm, verdant effect. The rest of the sheltered courtyard was planted as a citrus grove.

Wherever possible, Verde retained the irregularity of the original structure. Arches were kept slightly off center; walls weren't squared off or smoothed over. To make the doors on the ground floor more architecturally important, stone lintels were laid in an antique, peaked design.

The windows on the ground floor presented a unique problem. What is today the large main living room was originally a series of stalls, which opened out onto the

BAGNI

In most restorations, especially in the country, it's a good bet that bathrooms will need to be added. If there is any bathroom at all in the original house (and this implies running water, which is not a given), it is probably a cupboard-size room. Since space is generally not a problem in modern renovations, many architects and owners transform entire rooms into bathrooms rather than carving smaller spaces out of bigger rooms.

A preexisting arched niche was completely glassed in to form a shower at one end of the master bathroom in the Mondadori *masseria*.

Traditionally, Italian contractors think of bathrooms as sanitary and hygienic environments, so they often suggest covering the entire room in shiny, glazed tiles that prevent water damage and would be easy to keep spotless. But that much tiling isn't in keeping with the feeling of older homes.

Among the many design alternatives is colored cement. The pigments are mixed directly into the cement; once it's applied to floors and walls, it provides a beautiful yet virtually indestructible surface, resistant to wetness and humidity (see pages 252–53). Another option is terra-cotta tiles, for both inside shower stalls and as a sink surround. Although contractors may complain that they're too porous, they're perfectly fine to use in these situations.

Industrially produced glazed tiles are sometimes not rustic-looking enough for a country restoration; hand-painted majolica tiles can be a beautiful alternative. Towns such as Grottaglie in Puglia, Vietri in Campania, and Deruta in Umbria are full of artisans producing them. If their higher price presents a problem, they can be used just as a border to provide extra color and interest (see page 160). Still another option is to search out antique glazed tiles at salvage yards for backsplashes (see page 78).

One other note: Although most Americans question the need to install bidets in every bathroom, keep in mind that this is standard Italian practice, and if you eventually try to sell your home, the absence of one may seem quite odd to prospective buyers.

courtyard via two large archways. Rather than close the archways off with plate glass, a wrought-iron window frame, with small panels of glass, was created.

The interior of the house is simple and extremely comfortable. Special attention was given to the large and gracious bathrooms; ample and airy, each is a haven of luxuriousness. Rather than turn to the expected ceramic tile, which would have created a cold effect, warm-toned tinted cement paves the rooms and partly lines the walls.

If the interiors are almost monastic in their simplicity, the exteriors live and breathe the fragrant air of Puglia. A rose garden located at the back of the house is planted with more than fifty kinds of roses. The courtyard boasts lemons and oranges almost year-round and is home to an aviary of exotic parrots. A two-meter-high (80-inch) stone wall encloses a rigorously planted herb, vegetable, and flower garden.

An immense pool is hidden behind a thick planting of fragrant shrubs and local trees in front of the house. Bordered by salvaged paving stones, its edge slopes down gradually, creating a beachlike effect. A small inlet, just wide enough to swim through, leads through the bushes to a round Jacuzzi tucked out of sight.

TERRA-COTTA PIGMENTS were mixed into the cement, which was applied to the floor, tub, and sink support of a daughter's bathroom, above right. Below right: Colored cement defines the master bath as well. A pair of sinks is set into a masonry support, and the cupboards are made of latticework. The shower is located at the far end of the second room.

THE STONE ARCHED PORTICO that wraps around the courtyard, above, provides a shady respite from the strong southern sun. A stone sink is set into the pilaster on the right. The main part of the pool, opposite, is surrounded by antique *chianche* and connects to a Jacuzzi by a canal. The *masseria* can be seen in the background.

The *masseria* is surrounded by several outbuildings, all of which have been lovingly restored. They're almost obscured behind naturally grouped plantings; narrow pathways lead from the main house to the pool and the small stone buildings. These meandering trails, heady with the scent of lavender and thyme, lemon, and mint, are the very spirit of Puglia. ■

BUILDING AND DECORATIVE RESOURCES

ANTIQUES DEALERS

Anne Van Horenbeeck
Via Fosso Cupo 17/19
Cetona
Mobile: 0348 221 8643
(Specializing in garden
furniture and objects)

Vecchia Bottega Cagnan
Via Vecellio 5
Feltre (BL)
Tel: 0439 83677
(home on page 70)

ANTIQUES FAIRS AND FLEA MARKETS

Arezzo, Tuscany
First Sunday of every month
Tel: 0575 3770

Corte Maggiore
Mercatino dell'antiquariato e
cose d'altri tempi
First Sunday of every month
Tel: 0523 832 711

Cortona
Mostra mercato nazionale
del mobile antico
End of August through
beginning of September
Tel: 0575 630 353

Tivoli
Mostra mercato di anti-
quariato, collezionismo,
modernatirato e artigianato
Last Sunday of every month
Tel: 0736 256956

Piazzola sul Brenta
(5 miles from Padua)
Il Mercato di cose d'altri tempi
Last Sunday of every month
Tel: 0499 60 1019

Pissignano
Campello sul Clitunno,
Umbria
First Sunday of every month

Rome
Porta Portese
Every Sunday

Recanati, Marche
First Sunday and preceding
Saturday of every month
Tel: 0736 256 956

Trieste
Third Sunday of every
month
Tel: 040 679 6111

ARCHITECTS / DESIGNERS

Gretchen Alexander
San Marco 3788
30124 Venice
Tel: 041 277 0283
galexan@tin.it
(home on page 60)

Giampiero Bosoni
GA Architetti Associati
Via Aosta 2
20155 Milano
Tel: 02 336 00338
Fax: 02 331 04525
Studioga@flo.it
(home on page 48)

Sebastiano Brandolini
Via Olmetto 17
20123 Milan
Tel: 02 720 94704
(homes on pages 14, 24)

Daniele Cariani
Florence
Tel: 055 241 581
(home on page 140)

Claudio Palmi Caramel
Corso Milano 94
35139 Padua
Tel: 049 873 34444
Fax: 049 872 2374
(home on page 70)

Sophie Clarke
Casa Sorci
06044 Castel Ritaldi (PG)
Tel: 0743 51671
casasorci@libero.it
(garden design)
(home on page 166)

Giuseppe Carlo Ferrari
Via Carlo Giuseppe Merlo 3
20122 Milan
Tel: 02 781 502
Archgfer@tin.it
(home on page 24)

Domenico Minchilli
Via Baccina 59
00184 Rome
Tel/Fax: 06 683 2206
dminchilli@libero.it
(homes on pages 84, 130,
152, 190)

Andrea Truglio
Via del Corso 75
Rome
Tel: 06 361 1836
Fax: 06 361 2949
(home on page 224)

Marco Vidotto
Via dei Montanini 118
53100 Siena
Tel: 0577 285059
Fax: 0577 286149
mvidotto@comune.siena.it
(home on page 118)

Verde Visconti
Via Gregoriana 5
Rome
Tel: 06 699 0346
(home on page 258)

BATHROOM FIXTURES AND SUPPLIERS

Sanitari Orsolini
Località Centignano
Vignanello, Viterbo
Tel: 0761 754 222

Sanitari Ticchioni
Ponte San Giovanni
Perugia
Tel: 075 395 144

Sanitari Tombesi
Via del Rivo 206
Terni
Tel: 0744 300 529

CARPENTERS

Franco Agnoletto
Via Cal Piccole 39
31044 Montebelluna (TV)
Tel: 0423 609 496
(windows for home
on page 70)

Franco Calissano
Via Vesime 5
12070 Perletto (CN)
Tel: 0173 832 102
(home on page 48)

Ditta Augusto Capovilla
Santa Croce 853
Venice
Tel: 041 524 0759
(Specializing in antique
finishes and new millwork
using traditional techniques)
(home on page 60)

Argeo Magini
Vicolo Truzzi 79
Rome
Tel: 06 450 1324
(homes on pages 86, 152, 190)

Gianfranco Nisini
Vicolo degli Amatriciani 24
Rome
06 686 1868
(home on page 224)

Dario Rossi
Via S. Agnese 21
06010 San Secondo
Città di Castello
Tel: 075 857 8139
(Cabinets and windows)
(homes on pages 86, 152)

Stiltoce
Via Martiri 54
28883 Gravellona Toce (VB)
Tel: 0323 848 318
(home on page 24)

CEMENT TILES

**La San Giorgio dei
Fratelli Pecis**
Via Selva 38
24060 Zandobbio (BG)
Tel: 035 940 246
Fax: 035 944 276
(home on page 24)

Majolica Tiles

Ceramiche Sberna
Via Tiberina Centro 146
Deruta (PG)
Tel: 075 971 0206

Farnese
Piazza Farnese 52
Rome
Tel: 06 689 6109

Nicola Fasano
Via Caravaggio 45
Grottaglie (TA)
(home on page 258)

Metalsmiths

Gualtiero Brunellli e Peppino Moriconi
Pantalla (PG)
Tel: 075 888 176
(home on page 152)

Giancarlo Candeago
Località Pian da Lago 6
32043 Cortina d'Ampezzo (BL)
Tel: 0436 866 577
(home on page 70)

Robertino Terzuoli
Loc. Fornaci di Quinciano
(Monteroni d'Arbia)
Tel: 0577 374 709
(home on page 70)

Nurseries and Garden Suppliers

Flora 2000
Via Zenzalino Sud 19
Budrio
40054 Bologna,
Tel: 051 800 406
(Specializing in old breeds of fruit trees)

Vivaio Fratelli Ingegnoli
Corso Buenos Aires 54
20124 Milano
Tel: 02 294 00 403
(Seed catalog; will ship)

Vivaio Fratelli Margheriti
Chiusi (SI)
Tel: 0578 227 686
(Biggest nursery in central Italy)

Vivaio Guido degli'Innocenti
Via colle Ramole 7
Loc. Bottai, Tavarnuzze,
Firenze
Tel: 055 237 4547
(Best nursery in Italy for irises; good catalog)

Vivaio Tudergreen
Pian di Porto, Todi (PG)
Tel: 075 898 7128
(homes on pages 152, 178, 190)

Real Estate Agents

Agenzia Immobiliare I Tigli
Centro Commerciale COOP
Monteroni d'Arbia
Tel: 0577 373 067

Agenzia Immobiliare Locatelli
Piazza Dante 24/25
28831 Baveno (VB)
Tel: 0323 923 558
Fax: 0323 922 170
locatelli@locatelli.net
www.locatelli.net

Broker House srl
San Marco 2746
30124 Venice
Tel: 041 528 9379
(home on page 60)

Eurogroup 92
Via Gramsci, Lama
Perugia
Tel: 075 858 3542
www.eurogroup92.com

Real Estate CasAmbiente
Hermel, Johannes & Luisa
Massa Martana, Todi
Perugia
Tel: 075 894 73 61
www.casambiente.com
(some rentals and management as well)

Tuder Immobiliare
Claudio Santi
Battifolle 68
Loc. Ripaioli, Marsciano
Tel: 075 888 160

Salvage Yards; Old Building Materials

Enzo Belli
Via Toscana 49
Lerchi 06012
Città di Castello (PG)
Tel: 075 851 1062
(Good source for old doors)

Fiorillo
SS. Cassia Sud, km. 75, 84
Viterbo
Tel: 0761 263065
(Old fireplaces, tiles, portals, etc).

Fiorillo Chia
SS Ortana km. 17,200
Viterbo
Tel: 0761 74 31 56
(Old terra-cotta roof and floor tiles)

LACOLE, Fratelli Radicchi
Via Aretina 28
Lerchi 06012
Città di Castello (PG)
Tel: 075 851 1062
(Salvaged materials including beams, terra-cotta tiles, stone flooring)

Angelo Scopel
31030 Castelucco (TV)
Tel: 0337 502 317
(home on page 70)

Stone

Pelganta Antonio
Via Provinciale 186
28030 Trontano (NO)
Tel: 0324 242 24
Fax: 0342 481 869
(Supplied beola used in home on page 24)

Sergio Rigo
Via E. Muzio 10
20124 Milano
Tel: 02 6707 1849
Fax: 02 6707 5095
(Supplied marble in kitchen of home on page 24)

Stoves

Stufe, Feliciano Felici
Figline Di Prato
50040 Firenze
Tel: 0574 460 7 31
(Traditional terra-cotta stoves, fireplace fronts)

Stucco and Paint

Colorifcio Renzo Falleri
Via Tellini 2
20155 Milano
Tel: 02 331 01390

Edilia di Enrico Nali
San Marco 3511
30124 Venice
Tel: 041 241 1105
(Painting, stucco, decorating)
(home on page 60)

Fratelli Negri
Rome
Mobile: 0339 211 05 72
Tel: 06 688 91 857
(home on page 224)

Giuseppe Valentini
Via Larghe 1
S. Floriano
31033 Castelfranco V.to (TV)
Tel: 0336 668 191
(home on page 70)

Swimming Pools

Berg Piscine
Loc. Sentino
53040
Serre di Rapolan (SI)
Tel: 0577 704 705
Bergpisc@ats.it

MEGIP di Fabbri
Vicchio di Mugello (FI)
Tel: 055 844 8331

Piscine Castiglione
AIT srl
Via dell'Industria
Ponte San Giovanni (PG)
Tel: 075 599 0564
www.piscinecastiglione.it
(home on page 118)

Terra-Cotta Tiles

Fornace Calandrelli
Castelviscardo, Orvieto
Tel: 0763 361 656
(handmade floor tiles)

Fornace Giuliani
Castelviscardo, Orvieto
Tel: 0763 361 637
(handmade floor tiles)

Fornace Sugaroni
Castelviscardo, Orvieto
Tel: 0763 361 003
(handmade floor tiles)

Pratigliolmi srl.
Loc. Fruscola
Castelfranco di Sopra (AR)
Tel: 055 914 6063
(Tuscan-style terra-cotta roof
and floor tiles)

Terra-Cotta Planters and Vases

Fratelli Berti
Via dei Mille 5
Ripabianca (PG) 06053
Tel: 075 973 273

Cottura
10250 Santa Monica
Boulevard
Los Angeles, CA 90067
Tel: 310-277-3828

Trompe L'oeil / Decoration

Nina Eaton
334 Constitution Ave. NE
Washington, D.C. 20002
Tel: 202-675-0227

Ursula Franco
Via Monserrato 7
Rome
Tel: 06 688 02234

Matthew Imperiale
210 Thompson Street
New York, New York 10012
Tel: 212-982-8731

Jackie Tune
Località Maggiano
Pieve Scola
53031 Casole d'Elsa (SI)
Tel/Fax 0577 960 298
(home on page 118)

Upholsterers

Fabrizio Catoni
Via dei Coronari 223
Rome
Tel: 06 686 5020
(home on page 224)

Bruna Giontella
Voc. Sta. Maria 2
Camerata, Todi 06059 (PG)
Tel: 075 894 7148
(homes on pages 152, 190)

Sandro Pavone
Borgo Pio 33
Rome
Tel: 06 686 5087
(home on page 152)

Claudio Presotto
VIPRE
Via Cesare Cesariano 9
20154 Milano
Tel: 02 336 07046
(home on page 24)

Alessandro Vianello
Via Piave 31
30171 Venice
Tel: 041 980 989
(home on page 60)

Wood Floors

Giorgio Favero
Via delle Industrie 11
Trevignano (TV) 31033
Tel: 0423 670 177
(specializing in
antique floors)
(home on page 70)

Edil Artigiana di Giovanni Scremin
Via Postioma 20
31033 Castelfranco
Veneto (TV)
Tel/Fax: 0423 490 894
(old floors)
(home on page 70)

MPR s.n.c. di Mei Guido & Co.
Via A. Meucci 38-40
20090 Buccinasco (MI)
Tel: 02 457 08465
Fax: 02 457 08464

AN ITALIAN-ENGLISH GLOSSARY OF BUILDING TERMS

A due o più livelli – split-level

Acciaio – steel

Affittare – rent

Affresco – fresco, the technique of painting on wet plaster

Agente Immobiliare – real estate agent

Agriturismo – small hotel located on a working farm

Appaltatore edilizio – building contractor

Architetto – architect

Balcone – balcony

Battiscopa – baseboard

Borgo – village

Caldaia – boiler

Camino – fireplace

Cantiere – work site

Cantina –– cellar

Casa colonica – farmhouse

Cascina – country house

Catasto – land map tax registry

Cava – quarry

Cavo elettrico – power cable

Cemento – cement

Chianche – slabs of stone from Trani, in Puglia

Cisterna – storage tank, reservoir

Confine di proprietà – property line

Corrimano – railing (stair)

Cucina – kitchen

Disegno in scala – scale drawing

Dislivello – rise

Doccia – shower

Drenaggio – drainage

Elettricista – electrician

Falegname – carpenter, cabinetmaker

Ferro – iron

Ferro battuto – wrought iron

Finestra - window

Finto affresco – technique of painting on dry plaster, to resemble true fresco

Fossa biologica, fossa settica – septic tank

Geometra – surveyor

Ghiaia – gravel

Giardino – garden

Gradino – step

Grassello di calce – lime

Graticolato – trellis

Gronda – rain gutter

Idraulico – plumber

Imbiancatore – painter

Impresa – building contractor

Incassato – built-in (usually referring to built-in kitchen appliances)

Ingegnere – engineer

Intonaco – plaster

Lastra di vetro – windowpane

Lavabo – sink

Legno – wood

Loggia – portico

Lucernario – roof light, skylight

Malta – mortar

Marciapiede – walkway

Marmo – marble

Masseria – Large farm or collection of farms, found in southern Italy

Mattone – brick

Mattone refrattario – refractory brick

Mattonelle – tiles, or small bricks

Mattoni a vista – exposed brick

Muratori – stone or brick masons

Muratura in pietra – stonework

Muro – wall

Notaio – notary

Offerta di appalto – tender, bid

Palazzo – palace

Pavimentazione in legno – wood flooring

Pergola – arbor

Perizia – survey

Permesso – permit

Persiana – louvered shutter

Piano – story

Piazza – square, open space

Pietra a vista – exposed stone

Pilone – pylon

Piscina – pool

Pompa – pump

Porta – door

Portone – entrance door

Pozzo – well

Preventivo – quotation, estimate

Programma – schedule

Resigillare – repoint

Ringhiera – balcony railing

Riscaldamento – heating

Riscaldamento a pannelli radianti – radiant heating system

Riscaldamento a pavimento – underfloor heating

Roccia – rock

Rubinetto – faucet

Sabbia – sand

Sabbiatrice – sandblaster

Scala – stair, staircase

Scala a chiocciola – spiral staircase

Scuro – internal window shutter used to block out light

Serbatoio - reservoir

Servitù – easement, or right of way

Soggiorno – living room

Solaio – beam and slab floor (structural)

Solaio ventilato – ventilated structural ground floor

Strada – street, road

Stuccare – repoint

Tavola – wood board

Telaio – window frame

Terrazza - terrace

Termosifone - radiator

Trave – beam

Trullo – conical-shaped building, found in Puglia

Vincolato – listed as part of the country's cultural patrimony

ACKNOWLEDGMENTS

MANY FRIENDS AND COLLEAGUES gave freely of their time and effort to help track down the homes featured in this book. I would like to thank Elizabeth Kane at Clicquot, Lars Leicht and Elizabeth Koenig at Banfi, Elda Fabrizio at Dedar, Pieranna Cavalchini, Gigi Pescolderung, Mara Memo, Lorenzo Prando, Alice Feiring, and Rossella Speranza of Oldways Italia. Thanks also to Polly McBride for her assistance with photography.

I would also like to thank those who graciously opened their homes and shared their stories; their hospitality and generosity shines through on every page. They include David Leavitt and Mark Mitchell, Astier and Pietro Laureano, Katrin Arens, Ferenc and Candace Maté, Gianni Cacciarini and Daniele Cariani, Gaia and Giorgio Franchetti, Leonardo Mondadori, Contessa Loredan, Matteo Selvini and Katerina Weiss, Annalise and Roberto Da Sie, Peter and Heidi Pfefferkorn, Ghislaine and Annibale Brandolini d'Adda, Karen Wolman and Baruch Ben-Chorin, Stefania Puglisi Allegra and Alessandro Tedesco, Cornelia Lauf and Joseph Kosuth, Ursula Franco, Pam Moskow and Franco Piersanti, and all those who choose to remain anonymous. Thanks also to Merete Stenbock, whose home is pictured on pages 4–5, and to Betty and George Woodman, whose home graces our cover.

I couldn't have written this book without the assistance of the architects and designers who gave expert advice to me as well as to their clients: Marco Vidotto, Giampiero Bosoni, Andrea Truglio, Verde Visconti, Sebastiano Brandolini, Giuseppe Carlo Ferrari, Claudio Palmi Caramel, and Gretchen Alexander.

Heartfelt thanks to Laurie Orseck for patiently transforming my words into elegant prose. And to Susi Oberhelman for sorting through the mountains of photographs and choosing the best to appear in this book.

Thank you to my agents, Maureen and Eric Lasher, who had the excellent idea of sending some photos of my own home to Ann Bramson at Artisan. And of course, many thanks to Ann who, while looking at those photos, came up with the wonderful idea for this book.

This book owes everything to the extraordinary talent of Simon McBride, who went above and beyond the call of duty, traveling the length and breadth of Italy to capture these homes on film. His unerring eye has taught me much.

Final and biggest thanks of all go to my husband, Domenico Minchilli, who has shared his passion and knowledge of this topic dear to both our hearts. Without his love, support, and vision this book would not have been possible.